A HUNDRED YEARS
OF
ENGLISH POETRY

T0364327

A HUNDRED YEARS
OF
ENGLISH POETRY

Selected by

EDWARD B. POWLEY

CAMBRIDGE
AT THE UNIVERSITY PRESS
MCMXXXI

CAMBRIDGE
UNIVERSITY PRESS

University Printing House, Cambridge CB2 8BS, United Kingdom

Cambridge University Press is part of the University of Cambridge.

It furthers the University's mission by disseminating knowledge in the pursuit of
education, learning and research at the highest international levels of excellence.

www.cambridge.org
Information on this title: www.cambridge.org/9781107494428

© Cambridge University Press 1931

First published 1931
Re-issued 2015

A catalogue record for this publication is available from the British Library

ISBN 978-1-107-49442-8 Paperback

PREFACE

A Hundred Years of English Poetry is an Anthology designed to place before the reader a representative selection of English Poetry written during recent years.

What criteria govern the selection of poems for this Cambridge volume? A plain answer is possible.

For the poet, as for the philosopher, the 'universe of discourse' is wide. Each, philosopher and poet, may, as Plato recognised and said, be "a spectator of all time and all existence". About almost anything a poem may be penned; but not —*anyhow*! Every true poem *says something intelligibly*, expresses its message *with due regard for prosody* (it need not be alleged that there are no more rhythms and rimes to discover) and *makes an emotional appeal*.

Who, concerned for the good estate of English Literature, has not long been forced to the regrettable conclusion that most of the poems which appear in the periodical press or are collected and published in attractively bound volumes are unworthy of authorship? Here, thought is discernible, marred by awkwardness of expression; there, though the content be exiguous, the metrical workmanship possesses merit; more often than not, reason, rhythm and rime are all conspicuously absent—the product bearing every sign of undisciplined mind and lazy application. Even the genial *Punch* has to make a New Year resolution

> Not to condemn an age too much
> That lacks the mid-Victorian touch;
> But bravely suffer Georgian bards....

Why the editors of so many periodicals and certain publishers' readers should be so complacent lies beyond comprehension. The duty of teachers of English Literature is at least plain. The taste of the average boy and girl of sixteen in the matter of modern Poetry is sound enough. At the universities a few students of the shallow yet brilliant sort do cultivate an esotericism. Some of the aesthetes recover; others join the staffs of newspapers or set up coteries much given to mutual admiration. (These are they who add to the output of cheap perfume and crackling firework.) Outside the schools and universities—as any who have had experience of extra-mural teaching or broadcasting upon literary topics can tell—is a large public still perfectly competent to distinguish good Poetry from bad, yet much bemused by the new versifiers.

In these pages the task of rigorous exclusion of the poorer modern verse has not been shirked.

Palgrave's *Golden Treasury* introduced the Victorians to the "best original Lyrical pieces and Songs" from Tudor times to 1855. Entrenchment upon the scope of that justly famous collection has, in the planning of this book, been avoided; poets writing before 1855 are here included only if work of theirs be missing from Palgrave. Some 64 authors are represented by 106 poems and pieces. The reader may be disposed to contend that leaders such as Tennyson, Browning, Hardy, merit a greater proportion of representation than they receive. The only copyright difficulty encountered excludes Tennyson's ballad *The Revenge*; its length bars *A Dream of Fair Women*. Excerpts from Tennyson's plays or Browning's are not deemed essential. Hardy's great epic-drama *The Dynasts* asks an anthology to itself. Happily, at one shilling and sixpence, Messrs Macmillan have produced such a book—Mr J. H. Fowler's *Scenes from the Dynasts*. Here a single extract is printed, which, out of its context, does *not* represent Hardy's philosophy. Doubtless unknown writers have escaped attention, isolated sonnets of worth or lyrics of outstanding beauty been missed, because they have not appeared in the 'collected works of so and so'. Such oversight is inevitable. Indebtedness to other anthologists one gladly confesses. Mr Laurence Binyon's *Golden Treasury of Modern Lyrics* is especially admirable. But for many years to come no anthology of modern Poetry will claim to be definitive. Less than three years ago, one of the very greatest figures in our Literature, Thomas Hardy, died; Mr Kipling, Mr de la Mare, Mr Masefield, Sir Henry Newbolt are with us. By them and by younger aspirants Poetry of the right sort has been and is being written. If to re-appreciation of the merits of the great Victorian poets and towards appraisement of their successors this Anthology lead, its purpose will have been sufficiently answered.

EDWARD B. POWLEY

Authors' Club
November, 1930

ACKNOWLEDGMENTS

For permission to include copyright poems the editor offers his thanks to the following authors, publishers and holders of copyright: Messrs George Allen and Unwin, Ltd., for W. J. Cory's "Mimnermus"; Messrs G. Bell and Sons, Ltd., for Patmore's "Magna est Veritas"; Mr Laurence Binyon and the Proprietors of *The Times* for "For the Fallen"; Messrs Jonathan Cape, Ltd., for the late Mrs Mary Webb's "Farewell to Beauty"; Messrs Chatto and Windus for R. L. Stevenson's "Sing me a song..." and "Requiem", and A. W. E. O'Shaughnessy's "Ode"; Messrs Constable and Co., Ltd., for Mr Gordon Bottomley's "Calvary-Talk" and "Goneril's Lullaby"; to Mr Walter de la Mare for "Nod", "Off the Ground" and "Silver"; Messrs J. M. Dent and Sons, Ltd., for Mr G. K. Chesterton's "The Donkey"; Mr John Galsworthy for "Unknown"; Messrs William Heinemann, Ltd., for A. C. Swinburne's "When the hounds of spring" and "The Garden of Proserpine" and (with Mrs James Elroy Flecker's permission) for a selection from J. E. Flecker's "Hassan"; to Prof. A. E. Housman for "Epitaph on an Army of Mercenaries"; Messrs Ingpen and Grant for P. E. Thomas' "Adlestrop"; Messrs John Lane the Bodley Head, Ltd., for E. Dowson's "Vitae summa brevis...", for two extracts from the poems of Stephen Phillips, and for Mrs R. A. Taylor's "The Quietist"; Messrs Longmans, Green and Co., Ltd., for Andrew Lang's "The Odyssey"; Messrs Macmillan and Co., Ltd., for a selection from *The Dynasts*, and for five other selections from the poems of Thomas Hardy, for W. E. Henley's "Out of the night that covers me", and Mr Ralph Hodgson's "The Bells of Heaven", also for an extract from Tennyson's "The Ancient Sage" and for "Crossing the Bar", also for "The Land", from *A Diversity of Creatures*, and "Mine

Sweepers" from *Sea Warfare*, both reprinted by permission of Mr Rudyard Kipling; Messrs Martin Secker, Ltd., for three extracts from the poems of James Elroy Flecker; to Mr Wilfrid Meynell for Alice Meynell's "Renouncement" and for Francis Thompson's "The Hound of Heaven" and "The Kingdom of God", published by Messrs Burns, Oates and Washbourne, Ltd.; to Dr John Masefield for "Cargoes", "Beauty", "Fragment"; to Mr John Murray for Mrs Violet Jacob's "Tam i' the Kirk" and for Sir Henry Newbolt's "Drake's Drum" and "The Fighting Téméraire", taken, by permission, from *Poems New and Old*; to the Oxford University Press for Robert Bridges' "So sweet love seemed", for Austin Dobson's "A Ballad to Queen Elizabeth" reprinted by permission of Mr Alban Dobson, and for G. M. Hopkins' "Pied Beauty"; to Sir Owen Seaman for "To William Shakspeare"; to Miss F. M. Pomeroy for "Ad Naturam"; to Mr Siegfried Sassoon for "They" and "Memorial Tablet", published by Messrs William Heinemann, Ltd.; to Mrs E. A. Sharp for Fiona Macleod's "The Crescent Moon"; Messrs Sidgwick and Jackson, Ltd., for Mr E. C. Blunden's "Almswomen", Mr W. J. R. Turner's "Romance", Rupert Brooke's "The Hill" and "The Soldier", Mr J. Drinkwater's "Birthright" and for a selection from Dr John Masefield's "The Widow in the Bye Street", reprinted with the author's consent; to Dr W. R. Sorley for C. H. Sorley's "The Song of the Ungirt Runners"; to the Trustees of the estate of William Morris for "The Haystack in the Floods"; to Mr W. B. Yeats and Messrs T. Fisher Unwin, Ltd., for "The Lake Isle of Innisfree" from *Poems*; to Sir William Watson for leave to reproduce "World-Strangeness", "The Inexorable Law" and an extract from "Wordsworth's Grave".

Look thy last on all things lovely,
Every hour. Let no night
Seal thy sense in deathly slumber
Till to delight
Thou have paid thy utmost blessing;
Since that all things thou wouldst praise
Beauty took from those who loved them
In other days.

From: *Fare Well*

WALTER DE LA MARE

CONTENTS

HUNT, JAMES HENRY LEIGH, 1784–1859 . . page 1
Rondeau

PEACOCK, THOMAS LOVE, 1785–1866 . . . 2
The War-Song of Dinas Vawr

CARLYLE, THOMAS, 1795–1881 3
To-day

MACAULAY, THOMAS BABINGTON, 1800–1859 . 4
The Battle of Naseby

HAWKER, ROBERT STEPHEN, 1803–1875 . . 8
The Song of the Western Men

EMERSON, RALPH WALDO, 1803–1882 . . . 9
Brahma

BROWNING, ELIZABETH BARRETT, 1806–1861 . 10
(1) From *Sonnets from the Portuguese:* "How do I love thee?"; (2) *A Musical Instrument*

LONGFELLOW, HENRY WADSWORTH, 1807–1882 . 12
From *Tales of a Wayside Inn:* The Theologian's Tale— Torquemada

POE, EDGAR ALLAN, 1809–1849 18
To Helen

FITZGERALD, EDWARD, 1809–1883 . . . 19
Rubáiyát of Omar Khayyám of Naishápúr

TENNYSON, ALFRED, 1809–1892 32
1) *The Lady of Shalott*; (2) *The Lotos-Eaters: Choric Song*; (3) *Ulysses*; (4) *Break, break, break*; (5) From *The Princess:* "Tears, idle tears"; "Now sleeps the crimson petal"; (6) From *In Memoriam*; (7) From *The Ancient Sage*; (8) *Crossing the Bar*

HOLMES, OLIVER WENDELL, 1809–1894 . . 49
The Chambered Nautilus

BROWNING, ROBERT, 1812–1889 51
(1) *Johannes Agricola in Meditation*; (2) From *Pippa Passes*; (3) *The Lost Leader*; (4) From *Home-Thoughts, from Abroad*; (5) From *Fra Lippo Lippi*; (6) *Prospice*

BRONTË, EMILY, 1818–1848 61
"No coward soul is mine"

CLOUGH, ARTHUR HUGH, 1819–1861 . . page 62
    "Say not, the struggle nought availeth"

KINGSLEY, CHARLES, 1819–1875 63
    (1) *Airly Beacon*; (2) *Ode to the North-East Wind*

INGELOW, JEAN, 1820–1897 65
    The High Tide on the Coast of Lincolnshire (1571)

ARNOLD, MATTHEW, 1822–1888 71
    (1) From *Empedocles on Etna*; (2) *Requiescat*; (3) From
    Sohrab and Rustum; (4) *The Scholar-Gipsy*

CORY, WILLIAM JOHNSON, 1823–1892 . . . 82
    Mimnermus in Church

PATMORE, COVENTRY KERSEY DIGHTON, 1823–1896 83
    Magna est Veritas

ROSSETTI, DANTE GABRIEL, 1828–1882 . . 84
    From *The Choice*

ROSSETTI, CHRISTINA GEORGINA, 1830–1894 . 85
    (1) *Song*; (2) *A Birthday*; (3) *Up-hill*

DIXON, RICHARD WATSON, 1833–1900 . . . 87
    Song

THOMSON, JAMES, 1834–1882 87
    From *The City of Dreadful Night*

MORRIS, WILLIAM, 1834–1896 89
    The Haystack in the Floods

SWINBURNE, ALGERNON CHARLES, 1837–1909 . 94
    (1) From *Atalanta in Calydon*: "When the hounds of
    spring"; (2) *The Garden of Proserpine*

DOBSON, HENRY AUSTIN, 1840–1921 . . . 99
    A Ballad to Queen Elizabeth of the Spanish Armada

HARDY, THOMAS, 1840–1928 100
    (1) *Friends Beyond*; (2) *Lausanne. In Gibbon's old Garden*;
    (3) *In Time of "The Breaking of Nations"*; (4) *Afterwards*;
    (5) *Weathers*; (6) From the *After Scene* of *The Dynasts*

O'SHAUGHNESSY, ARTHUR WILLIAM EDGAR, 1844–
1881 106
    Ode

HOPKINS, GERARD MANLEY, 1844–1889 . . 108
    Pied Beauty

LANG, ANDREW, 1844–1912 109
    The Odyssey

BRIDGES, ROBERT SEYMOUR, 1844–1930 . . 110
    "So sweet love seemed"

MEYNELL, ALICE CHRISTIANA, 1847–1922 . . 111
    Renouncement

xii

HENLEY, WILLIAM ERNEST, 1849–1903 . page 111
  "Out of the night that covers me"

STEVENSON, ROBERT LOUIS, 1850–1894 . . 112
  (1) "Sing me a song of a lad that is gone"; (2) *Requiem*

SHARP, WILLIAM (FIONA MACLEOD), 1856–1905 . 113
  The Crescent Moon

WATSON, (SIR) WILLIAM, 1858– 114
  (1) From *Wordsworth' Grave*; (2) *World-Strangeness*;
  (3) *The Inexorable Law:* "We, too, shall pass"

THOMPSON, FRANCIS, 1859–1907 . . . 116
  (1) *The Hound of Heaven*; (2) *The Kingdom of God*

HOUSMAN, ALFRED EDWARD, 1859– . . . 122
  Epitaph on an Army of Mercenaries

SEAMAN, (SIR) OWEN, 1861– 123
  To William Shakspeare

NEWBOLT, (SIR) HENRY JOHN, 1862– . . 124
  (1) *Drake's Drum*; (2) *The Fighting Téméraire*

JACOB, VIOLET, 1863– 127
  Tam i' the Kirk

KIPLING, RUDYARD, 1865– 128
  (1) *The Land:* "When Julius Fabricius"; (2) *Mine Sweepers*

YEATS, WILLIAM BUTLER, 1865– . . . 133
  The Lake Isle of Innisfree

DOWSON, ERNEST, 1867–1900 . . . 134
  Vitae summa brevis spem nos vetat incohare longam

GALSWORTHY, JOHN, 1867– 134
  Unknown: "You who had worked in perfect ways"

PHILLIPS, STEPHEN, 1864–1915 . . . 136
  (1) From *Paolo and Francesca:* Act I and Act IV;
  (2) *Shakespeare*

BINYON, LAURENCE, 1869– 142
  For the Fallen: "With proud thanksgiving"

HODGSON, RALPH, 1872– 143
  The Bells of Heaven

DE LA MARE, WALTER, 1873– . . . 143
  (1) *Nod*; (2) *Off the Ground*; (3) *Silver*

BOTTOMLEY, GORDON, 1874– . . . 148
  (1) *Calvary-Talk*; (2) From *King Lear's Wife: Goneril's Lullaby*

CHESTERTON, GILBERT KEITH, 1874– . . 151
  The Donkey

xiii

TAYLOR, RACHEL ANNAND, 1876– . . page 152
 The Quietist

MASEFIELD, JOHN, 1878– 152
 (1) *Cargoes*; (2) *Beauty*; (3) From *Fragments*; (4) From *The Widow in the Bye Street*

THOMAS, PHILIP EDWARD, 1878 1917 . . . 158
 Adlestrop

WEBB, MARY, 1881–1927 159
 Farewell to Beauty

DRINKWATER, JOHN, 1882– 160
 Birthright

FLECKER, HERMAN (JAMES) ELROY, 1884–1915 . 161
 (1) *To a Poet a Thousand Years Hence*; (2) From *Hassan: Act V, Sc. 2*; (3) *The Old Ships*

SASSOON, SIEGFRIED LORAINE, 1886– . . . 166
 (1) "*They*"; (2) *Memorial Tablet (Great War)*

BROOKE, RUPERT, 1887–1915 167
 (1) *The Hill*; (2) *The Soldier*

TURNER, WALTER JAMES REDFERN, 1889– . . 168
 Romance

POMEROY, FLORENCE MARY, 1892– . . . 169
 Ad Naturam

SORLEY, CHARLES HAMILTON, 1895–1915 . . 170
 The Song of the Ungirt Runners

BLUNDEN, EDMUND CHARLES, 1896– . . . 171
 Almswomen

Index of First Lines 173

A HUNDRED YEARS

OF

ENGLISH POETRY

HUNT, James Henry Leigh

JAMES HENRY LEIGH HUNT (1784–1859) was of American
extraction. He was born at Southgate, Middlesex, and
educated at Christ's Hospital. As editor of *The Examiner*,
he was prosecuted for criticising flogging in the army and
imprisoned for attacking the Prince Regent. Hunt introduced Keats and Shelley to each other; and his paper
commended those young poets to the public. Shelley,
till his death in 1822, befriended him. With Byron,
Hunt's connection was less happy. His long straitened
circumstances were relieved by a Civil List pension in
1847. This discerning critic, though his poetical works
are largely unread, has his place in the revival of Roman-
ticism in English poetry.

Rondeau

JENNY kissed me when we met,
   Jumping from the chair she sat in;
Time, you thief, who love to get
   Sweets into your list, put that in!
Say I'm weary, say I'm sad,
   Say that health and wealth have missed me,
Say I'm growing old, but add,
   Jenny kissed me.

PEACOCK, Thomas Love

THOMAS LOVE PEACOCK (1785–1866) was born at Weymouth and privately educated. He was introduced by a publisher to Shelley whose friend he became. Peacock found his *métier* in writing fantastic-satiric novels of which *Nightmare Abbey* is probably the best known. He received unexpected appointment at India House. Peacock has left reminiscences and letters of Shelley.

The War-Song of Dinas Vawr

THE mountain sheep are sweeter,
But the valley sheep are fatter;
We therefore deemed it meeter
To carry off the latter.
We made an expedition;
We met an host, and quelled it;
We forced a strong position,
And killed the men who held it.

On Dyfed's richest valley,
Where herds of kine were browsing,
We made a mighty sally,
To furnish our carousing.
Fierce warriors rushed to meet us;
We met them, and o'erthrew them:
They struggled hard to beat us;
But we conquered them, and slew them.

As we drove our prize at leisure,
The king marched forth to catch us:
His rage surpassed all measure,
But his people could not match us.
He fled to his hall-pillars;
And, ere our force we led off,
Some sacked his house and cellars,
While others cut his head off.

We there, in strife bewildering,
Spilt blood enough to swim in:
We orphaned many children,
And widowed many women.
The eagles and the ravens
We glutted with our foemen;
The heroes and the cravens,
The spearmen and the bowmen.

We brought away from battle,
And much their land bemoaned them,
Two thousand head of cattle,
And the head of him who owned them:
Ednyfed, King of Dyfed,
His head was borne before us;
His wine and beasts supplied our feasts,
And his overthrow, our chorus.

CARLYLE, Thomas

THOMAS CARLYLE (1795–1881) was born at Ecclefechan,
Annandale. He was educated at the village school, Annan
Grammar School and Edinburgh University—he tramped
the hundred miles to keep his first term! He deserted
schoolmastering for literature. No publisher would accept *Sartor Resartus*. The dyspeptic Carlyle persisted,
produced the MS. of the first volume of *The History of the
French Revolution*, lent it to J. S. Mill. It was accidentally
burned. Carlyle rewrote and completed the MS., making
his reputation. *Heroes and Hero-Worship, Past and
Present, Letters and Speeches of Oliver Cromwell, The Life
of John Sterling* and *The Life of Frederick the Great* are
among Carlyle's best known works, which, in thought and
style, are ruggedly Germanic.

To-day

So here hath been dawning
Another blue day.
Think, wilt thou let it
Slip useless away?

Out of eternity
This new day is born;
Into eternity,
At night, will return.

Behold it aforetime
No eye ever did:
So soon it forever
From all eyes is hid.

Here hath been dawning
Another blue day.
Think, wilt thou let it
Slip useless away?

MACAULAY, Thomas Babington, Lord

THOMAS BABINGTON MACAULAY—1st baron Macaulay—
(1800–1859), the son of Zachary Macaulay, was born at
Rothley Temple, Leicestershire, and educated privately
and at Trinity College, Cambridge. He wrote for *The
Edinburgh Review*; then combined literature and politics.
The Lays of Ancient Rome, *The Armada* and similar poems
are known to the schoolboy; so too are such essays as those
on *Clive*, *Warren Hastings* and *Chatham*. His great un-
finished *History of England* is his masterpiece. About
two years before death he received a barony. He is buried
in Westminster Abbey.

The Battle of Naseby

By Obadiah Bind-their-kings-in-chains-and-their-nobles
-with-links-of-iron, Serjeant in Ireton's Regiment

OH! wherefore come ye forth, in triumph from the
North,
With your hands, and your feet, and your rai-
ment all red?
And wherefore doth your rout sent forth a joyous
shout?
And whence be the grapes of the wine-press
which ye tread?

4

Oh evil was the root, and bitter was the fruit,
    And crimson was the juice of the vintage that we
        trod;
For we trampled on the throng of the haughty and
    the strong,
    Who sate in the high places, and slew the saints
        of God.

It was about the noon of a glorious day of June,
    That we saw their banners dance, and their
        cuirasses shine,
And the Man of Blood was there, with his long
    essenced hair,
    And Astley, and Sir Marmaduke, and Rupert of
        the Rhine.

Like a servant of the Lord, with his Bible and his
        sword,
    The General rode along us to form us to the fight,
When a murmuring sound broke out, and swell'd
        into a shout,
    Among the godless horsemen upon the tyrant's
        right.

And hark! like the roar of the billows on the shore,
    The cry of battle rises along their charging line!
For God! for the Cause! for the Church! for the
    Laws!
    For Charles King of England, and Rupert of the
        Rhine!

The furious German comes, with his clarions and
    his drums,
    His bravoes of Alsatia, and pages of Whitehall;
They are bursting on our flanks. Grasp your pikes,
    close your ranks;
    For Rupert never comes but to conquer or to
        fall.

They are here! They rush on! We are broken!
 We are gone!
  Our left is borne before them like stubble on the
  blast.
O Lord, put forth thy might! O Lord, defend the
 right!
  Stand back to back, in God's name, and fight it to
  the last.

Stout Skippon hath a wound; the centre hath given
 ground:
  Hark! hark!—What means the trampling of
  horsemen on our rear?
Whose banner do I see, boys? 'Tis he, thank God
 'tis he, boys.
  Bear up another minute: brave Oliver is here.

Their heads all stooping low, their points all in a
 row,
  Like a whirlwind on the trees, like a deluge on
  the dykes,
Our cuirassiers have burst on the ranks of the
 Accurst,
  And at a shock have scattered the forest of his
  pikes.

Fast, fast, the gallants ride, in some safe nook to hide
 Their coward heads, predestined to rot on
 Temple Bar:
And he—he turns, he flies:—shame on those cruel
 eyes
  That bore to look on torture, and dare not look
  on war.

Ho! comrades, scour the plain; and, ere ye strip the
 slain,
  First give another stab to make your search
  secure,

6

Then shake from sleeves and pockets their broad-
  pieces and lockets,
  The tokens of the wanton, the plunder of the
    poor.

Fools! your doublets shone with gold, and your
  hearts were gay and bold,
  When you kissed your lily hands to your lemans
    to-day;
And to-morrow shall the fox, from her chambers in
  the rocks,
  Lead forth her tawny cubs to howl above the prey.

Where be your tongues that late mocked at heaven
  and hell and fate,
  And the fingers that once were so busy with your
    blades,
Your perfum'd satin clothes, your catches and your
  oaths,
  Your stage-plays and your sonnets, your dia-
    monds and your spades?

Down, down, for ever down with the mitre and the
  crown,
  With the Belial of the Court, and the Mammon
    of the Pope;
There is woe in Oxford Halls; there is wail in
  Durham's Stalls:
  The Jesuit smites his bosom: the Bishop rends
    his cope.

And She of the seven hills shall mourn her children's
  ills,
  And tremble when she thinks on the edge of
    England's sword;
And the Kings of earth in fear shall shudder when
  they hear
  What the hand of God hath wrought for the
    Houses and the Word.

HAWKER, Robert Stephen

ROBERT STEPHEN HAWKER (1803–1875) was born at Stoke
Damerel, Devon, educated at Liskeard and Cheltenham
Grammar Schools and Pembroke College, Oxford. He
took Anglican orders and, in his last hours, turned Roman
Catholic. Of a quantity of verse the following ballad,
lacking historical warrant, is best known.

The Song of the Western Men

A GOOD sword and a trusty hand!
　A merry heart and true!
King James's men shall understand
　What Cornish lads can do.

And have they fixed the where and when?
　And shall Trelawny die?
Here's twenty thousand Cornish men
　Will know the reason why!

Out spake their captain brave and bold,
　A merry wight was he:
"If London Tower were Michael's hold,
　We'll set Trelawny free!

"We'll cross the Tamar, land to land,
　The Severn is no stay,—
With 'one and all,' and hand in hand,
　And who shall bid us nay?

"And when we come to London Wall,
　A pleasant sight to view,
Come forth! Come forth, ye cowards all,
　Here's men as good as you.

"Trelawny he's in keep and hold,
　Trelawny he may die;
But here's twenty thousand Cornish bold
　Will know the reason why!"

EMERSON, Ralph Waldo

RALPH WALDO EMERSON (1803–1882) was born at Boston, Massachusetts. He studied at Harvard, became a minister, grew unorthodox and resigned his charge. Visiting Europe, he met Carlyle and other leaders of thought. Returning to the U.S.A., Emerson lectured widely. He revisited Europe in 1847, meeting and greatly influencing Clough. His essays are well known.

Brahma

IF the red slayer think he slays,
  Or if the slain think he is slain,
They know not well the subtle ways
  I keep, and pass, and turn again.

Far or forgot to me is near;
  Shadow and sunlight are the same;
The vanished gods to me appear;
  And one to me are shame and fame.

They reckon ill who leave me out;
  When me they fly, I am the wings;
I am the doubter and the doubt,
  And I the hymn the Brahmin sings.

The strong gods pine for my abode,
  And pine in vain the sacred Seven,
But thou, meek lover of the good!
  Find me, and turn thy back on heaven.

BROWNING, Elizabeth Barrett

ELIZABETH BARRETT BROWNING (1806–1861), born at Burn Hall, Durham, was privately educated. A translation of Æschylus' *Prometheus Bound* secured her recognition. That, together with *The Cry of the Children* and *Sonnets from the Portuguese*, were her outstanding achievements, before marriage to Robert Browning. *Casa Guidi Windows* and *Aurora Leigh* appeared later.

From *Sonnets from the Portuguese*

How do I love thee? Let me count the ways.
I love thee to the depth and breadth and height
My soul can reach, when feeling out of sight
For the ends of Being and ideal Grace.
I love thee to the level of everyday's
Most quiet need, by sun and candlelight.
I love thee freely, as men strive for Right;
I love thee purely, as they turn from Praise.
I love thee with the passion put to use
In my old griefs, and with my childhood's faith.
I love thee with a love I seemed to lose
With my lost saints,—I love thee with the breath,
Smiles, tears, of all my life!—and, if God choose,
I shall but love thee better after death.

A Musical Instrument

What was he doing, the great god Pan,
    Down in the reeds by the river?
Spreading ruin and scattering ban,
Splashing and paddling with hoofs of a goat,
And breaking the golden lilies afloat
    With the dragon-fly on the river.

He tore out a reed, the great god Pan,
    From the deep cool bed of the river:
The limpid water turbidly ran,
And the broken lilies a-dying lay,
And the dragon-fly had fled away,
    Ere he brought it out of the river.

High on the shore sate the great god Pan,
　　While turbidly flowed the river;
And hacked and hewed as a great god can,
With his hard bleak steel at the patient reed,
Till there was not a sign of a leaf indeed
　　To prove it fresh from the river.

He cut it short, did the great god Pan
　　(How tall it stood in the river!),
Then drew the pith, like the heart of a man,
Steadily from the outside ring,
And notched the poor dry empty thing
　　In holes, as he sate by the river.

"This is the way," laughed the great god Pan
　　(Laughed while he sate by the river),
"The only way, since gods began
To make sweet music, they could succeed."
Then, dropping his mouth to a hole in the reed,
　　He blew in power by the river.

Sweet, sweet, sweet, O Pan!
　　Piercing sweet by the river!
Blinding sweet, O great god Pan!
The sun on the hill forgot to die,
And the lilies revived, and the dragon-fly
　　Came back to dream on the river.

Yet half a beast is the great god Pan,
　　To laugh as he sits by the river,
Making a poet out of a man:
The true gods sigh for the cost and pain,—
For the reed which grows nevermore again
　　As a reed with the reeds in the river.

LONGFELLOW, Henry Wadsworth

HENRY WADSWORTH LONGFELLOW (1807–1882), born at Portland, Maine, lived as a boy in his native town, entered Bowdoin College, Brunswick, Maine, travelled in Europe and took up a professorship at his college. In 1836 Longfellow received appointment at Harvard and taught there till 1854. The much hackneyed *Wreck of the Hesperus*, *The Village Blacksmith* and *Excelsior* were early work. *Evangeline*, *Hiawatha*, *The Courtship of Miles Standish* and *Tales of a Wayside Inn* are well known. Longfellow's travels in Europe incalculably influenced his outlook. His facility of versification and simplicity of thought made him an excellent narrator; if his poetry never soars, it seldom fails to charm.

From *Tales of a Wayside Inn*

The Theologian's Tale

Torquemada

IN the heroic days when Ferdinand
And Isabella ruled the Spanish land,
And Torquemada, with his subtle brain,
Ruled them, as Grand Inquisitor of Spain,
In a great castle near Valladolid,
Moated and high and by fair woodlands hid,
There dwelt, as from the chronicles we learn,
An old Hidalgo, proud and taciturn,
Whose name has perished, with his towers of stone,
And all his actions save this one alone;
This one, so terrible, perhaps 'twere best
If it, too, were forgotten with the rest;
Unless, perchance, our eyes can see therein
The martyrdom triumphant o'er the sin;
A double picture, with its gloom and glow,
The splendour overhead, the death below.

This sombre man counted each day as lost
On which his feet no sacred threshold crossed;
And when he chanced the passing Host to meet,
He knelt and prayed devoutly in the street;

Oft he confessed; and with each mutinous thought,
As with wild beasts at Ephesus, he fought.
In deep contrition scourged himself in Lent,
Walked in processions, with his head down bent;
At plays of Corpus Christi oft was seen,
And on Palm Sunday bore his bough of green.
His only pastime was to hunt the boar
Through tangled thickets of the forest hoar,
Or with his jingling mules to hurry down
To some grand bull-fight in the neighbouring town,
Or in the crowd with lighted taper stand,
When Jews were burned, or banished from the
  land.
Then stirred within him a tumultuous joy;
The demon whose delight is to destroy
Shook him, and shouted with a trumpet tone,
"Kill! kill! and let the Lord find out his own!"

And now, in that old castle in the wood,
His daughters in the dawn of womanhood,
Returning from their convent school, had made
Resplendent with their bloom the forest shade,
Reminding him of their dead mother's face,
When first she came into that gloomy place,—
A memory in his heart as dim and sweet
As moonlight in a solitary street,
Where the same rays, that lift the sea, are thrown
Lovely but powerless upon walls of stone.
These two fair daughters of a mother dead
Were all the dream had left him as it fled.
A joy at first, and then a growing care,
As if a voice within him cried, "Beware!"
A vague presentiment of impending doom,
Like ghostly footsteps in a vacant room,
Haunted him day and night; a formless fear
That death to some one of his house was near,
With dark surmises of a hidden crime,
Made life itself a death before its time.

Jealous, suspicious, with no sense of shame,
A spy upon his daughters he became;
With velvet slippers, noiseless on the floors,
He glided softly through half-open doors;
Now in the room, and now upon the stair,
He stood beside them ere they were aware;
He listened in the passage when they talked,
He watched them from the casement when they
       walked,
He saw the gipsy haunt the river's side,
He saw the monk among the cork-trees glide;
And tortured by the mystery and the doubt
Of some dark secret, past his finding out,
Baffled he paused; then, reassured again
Pursued the flying phantom of his brain.
He watched them even when they knelt in church;
And then, descending lower in his search,
Questioned the servants, and with eager eyes
Listened incredulous to their replies;
The gipsy? none had seen her in the wood!
The monk? a mendicant in search of food!

At length the awful revelation came,
Crushing at once his pride of birth and name,
The hopes his yearning bosom forward cast,
And the ancestral glories of the past;
All fell together, crumbling in disgrace,
A turret rent from battlement to base.
His daughters talking in the dead of night
In their own chamber, and without a light,
Listening, as he was wont, he overheard,
And learned the dreadful secret, word by word;
And hurrying from his castle, with a cry
He raised his hands to the unpitying sky,
Repeating one dread word, till bush and tree
Caught it, and shuddering answered, "Heresy!"

Wrapped in his cloak, his hat drawn o'er his face,
Now hurrying forward, now with lingering pace,

He walked all night the alleys of his park,
With one unseen companion in the dark,
The demon who within him lay in wait,
And by his presence turned his love to hate,
For ever muttering in an undertone,
"Kill! kill! and let the Lord find out his own!"

Upon the morrow, after early Mass,
While yet the dew was glistening on the grass,
And all the woods were musical with birds,
The old Hidalgo, uttering fearful words,
Walked homeward with the Priest, and in his room
Summoned his trembling daughters to their doom
When questioned, with brief answers they replied
Nor when accused evaded or denied;
Expostulations, passionate appeals,
All that the human heart most fears or feels,
In vain the Priest with earnest voice essayed;
In vain the father threatened, wept, and prayed;
Until at last he said, with haughty mien,
"The Holy Office, then, must intervene!"

And now the Grand Inquisitor of Spain,
With all the fifty horsemen of his train,
His awful name resounding, like the blast
Of funeral trumpets, as he onward passed,
Came to Valladolid, and there began
To harry the rich Jews with fire and ban.
To him the Hidalgo went, and at the gate
Demanded audience on affairs of state,
And in a secret chamber stood before
A venerable greybeard of fourscore,
Dressed in the hood and habit of a friar;
Out of his eyes flashed a consuming fire,
And in his hand the mystic horn he held,
Which poison and all noxious charms dispelled.
He heard in silence the Hidalgo's tale,
Then answered in a voice that made him quail:

"Son of the Church! when Abraham of old
To sacrifice his only son was told,
He did not pause to parley nor protest,
But hastened to obey the Lord's behest.
In him it was accounted righteousness;
The Holy Church expects of thee no less!"

A sacred frenzy seized the father's brain,
And Mercy from that hour implored in vain.
Ah! who will e'er believe the words I say?
His daughters he accused, and the same day
They both were cast into the dungeon's gloom,
That dismal antechamber of the tomb,
Arraigned, condemned, and sentenced to the flame,
The secret torture and the public shame.

Then to the Grand Inquisitor once more
The Hidalgo went, more eager than before,
And said: "When Abraham offered up his son,
He clave the wood wherewith it might be done.
By his example taught, let me too bring
Wood from the forest for my offering!"
And the deep voice, without a pause, replied:
"Son of the Church! by faith now justified,
Complete thy sacrifice, even as thou wilt;
The Church absolves thy conscience from all guilt!"

Then this most wretched father went his way
Into the woods, that round his castle lay,
Where once his daughters in their childhood played
With their young mother in the sun and shade.
Now all the leaves had fallen; the branches bare
Made a perpetual moaning in the air,
And screaming from their eyries overhead
The ravens sailed athwart the sky of lead.
With his own hands he lopped the boughs and bound
Fagots, that crackled with foreboding sound,
And on his mules, caparisoned and gay
With bells and tassels, sent them on their way.

Then with his mind on one dark purpose bent,
Again to the Inquisitor he went,
And said: "Behold the fagots I have brought;
And now, lest my atonement be as nought,
Grant me one more request, one last desire,—
With my own hands to light the funeral fire!"
And Torquemada answered from his seat,
"Son of the Church! Thine offering is complete;
Her servants through all ages shall not cease
To magnify thy deed. Depart in peace!"

Upon the market-place, builded of stone
The scaffold rose, whereon Death claimed his own.
At the four corners, in stern attitude,
Four statues of the Hebrew Prophets stood,
Gazing with calm indifference in their eyes
Upon this place of human sacrifice,
Round which was gathering fast the eager crowd,
With clamour of voices dissonant and loud;
And every roof and window was alive
With restless gazers, swarming like a hive.

The church-bells tolled, the chant of monks drew
near,
Loud trumpets stammered forth their notes of fear,
A line of torches smoked along the street,
There was a stir, a rush, a tramp of feet,
And with its banners floating in the air,
Slowly the long procession crossed the square,
And, to the statues of the Prophets bound,
The victims stood, with fagots piled around.
Then all the air a blast of trumpets shook,
And louder sang the monks with bell and book,
And the Hidalgo, lofty, stern, and proud,
Lifted his torch, and, bursting through the crowd,
Lighted in haste the fagots, and then fled,
Lest those imploring eyes should strike him dead!

O pitiless skies! why did your clouds retain
For peasants' fields their floods of hoarded rain?

O pitiless earth! why opened no abyss
To bury in its chasm a crime like this?

That night, a mingled column of fire and smoke
From the dark thickets of the forest broke,
And, glaring o'er the landscape leagues away,
Made all the fields and hamlets bright as day.
Wrapped in a sheet of flame the castle blazed,
And as the villagers in terror gazed,
They saw the figure of that cruel knight
Lean from a window in the turret's height,
His ghastly face illumined with the glare,
His hands upraised above his head in prayer,
Till the floor sank beneath him, and he fell
Down the black hollow of that burning well.

Three centuries and more above his bones
Have piled the oblivious years like funeral stones;
His name has perished with him, and no trace
Remains on earth of his afflicted race;
But Torquemada's name, with clouds o'ercast,
Looms in the distant landscape of the Past,
Like a burnt tower upon a blackened heath,
Lit by the fires of burning woods beneath!

POE, Edgar Allan

EDGAR ALLAN POE (1809–1849), born in Boston, Massachusetts, was orphaned at the age of two. He was educated in England and Virginia. Poe earned his livelihood at journalism, producing powerful tales and verse for poor pay. *The Raven* brought him in two pounds only.

To Helen

HELEN, thy beauty is to me
Like those Nicean barks of yore,
That gently, o'er a perfumed sea,
The weary, way-worn wanderer bore
To his own native shore.

On desperate seas long wont to roam,
Thy hyacinth hair, thy classic face,
Thy Naiad airs have brought me home
To the glory that was Greece,
And the grandeur that was Rome.

Lo! in yon brilliant window niche
How statue-like I see thee stand,
The agate lamp within thy hand!
Ah, Psyche, from the regions which
Are Holy-Land!

FITZGERALD, Edward

EDWARD FITZGERALD (1809–1883) was born at Bredfield,
near Woodbridge, Suffolk, and educated at the Grammar
School at Bury St Edmunds and Trinity College, Cambridge. He rendered, rather than translated into English,
Spanish, Greek and Persian originals.

Rubáiyát of Omar Khayyám of Naishápúr

I

AWAKE! for Morning in the Bowl of Night
Has flung the Stone that puts the Stars to Flight:
  And Lo! the Hunter of the East has caught
The Sultán's Turret in a Noose of Light.

II

Dreaming when Dawn's Left Hand was in the Sky
I heard a Voice within the Tavern cry,
  "Awake, my Little ones, and fill the Cup
"Before Life's Liquor in its Cup be dry."

III

And, as the Cock crew, those who stood before
The Tavern shouted—"Open then the Door!
  "You know how little while we have to stay,
"And, once departed, may return no more."

IV

Now the New Year reviving old Desires,
The thoughtful Soul to Solitude retires,
　　Where the WHITE HAND OF MOSES on the Bough
Puts out, and Jesus from the ground suspires.

V

Irám indeed is gone with all its Rose,
And Jamshýd's Sev'n-ring'd Cup where no one
　　　　knows;
　　But still the Vine her ancient Ruby yields,
And still a Garden by the Water blows.

VI

And David's Lips are lock't; but in divine
High-piping Péhlevi, with "Wine! Wine! Wine!
　　"*Red* Wine!"—the Nightingale cries to the Rose
That yellow Cheek of hers to'incarnadine.

VII

Come, fill the Cup, and in the Fire of Spring
The Winter Garment of Repentance fling:
　　The Bird of Time has but a little way
To fly—and Lo! the Bird is on the Wing.

VIII

And look—a thousand Blossoms with the Day
Woke—and a thousand scatter'd into Clay:
　　And this first Summer Month that brings the
　　　　Rose
Shall take Jamshýd and Kaikobád away.

IX

But come with old Khayyám, and leave the Lot
Of Kaikobád and Kaikhosrú forgot:
　　Let Rustum lay about him as he will,
Or Hátim Tai cry Supper—heed them not.

20

X

With me along some Strip of Herbage strown
That just divides the desert from the sown,
    Where name of Slave and Sultán scarce is known,
And pity Sultán Máhmúd on his Throne.

XI

Here with a Loaf of Bread beneath the Bough,
A Flask of Wine, a Book of Verse—and Thou
    Beside me singing in the Wilderness—
And Wilderness is Paradise enow.

XII

"How sweet is mortal Sovranty!"—think some:
Others—"How blest the Paradise to come!"
    Ah, take the Cash in hand and wave the Rest;
Oh, the brave Music of a *distant* Drum!

XIII

Look to the Rose that blows about us—"Lo,
"Laughing," she says, "into the World I blow:
    "At once the silken Tassel of my Purse
"Tear, and its Treasure on the Garden throw."

XIV

The Worldly Hope men set their Hearts upon
Turns Ashes—or it prospers; and anon,
    Like Snow upon the Desert's dusty Face
Lighting a little Hour or two—is gone.

XV

And those who husbanded the Golden Grain,
And those who flung it to the Winds like Rain,
    Alike to no such aureate Earth are turn'd
As, buried once, Men want dug up again.

XVI

Think, in this batter'd Caravanserai
Whose Doorways are alternate Night and Day,
    How Sultán after Sultán with his Pomp
Abode his Hour or two, and went his way.

XVII

They say the Lion and the Lizard keep
The Courts where Jamshýd gloried and drank deep:
    And Bahrám, that great Hunter—the Wild Ass
Stamps o'er his Head, and he lies fast asleep.

XVIII

I sometimes think that never blows so red
The Rose as where some buried Cæsar bled;
    That every Hyacinth the Garden wears
Dropt in its Lap from some once lovely Head.

XIX

And this delightful Herb whose tender Green
Fledges the River's Lip on which we lean—
    Ah, lean upon it lightly! for who knows
From what once lovely Lip it springs unseen!

XX

Ah, my Belovéd, fill the Cup that clears
TO-DAY of past Regrets and future Fears—
    To-morrow?—Why, To-morrow I may be
Myself with Yesterday's Sev'n Thousand Years.

XXI

Lo! some we loved, the loveliest and best
That Time and Fate of all their Vintage prest,
    Have drunk their Cup a Round or two before,
And one by one crept silently to Rest.

XXII

And we, that now make merry in the Room
They left, and Summer dresses in new Bloom,
  Ourselves must we beneath the Couch of Earth
Descend, ourselves to make a Couch—for whom?

XXIII

Ah, make the most of what we yet may spend,
Before we too into the Dust descend;
  Dust into Dust, and under Dust, to lie,
Sans Wine, sans Song, sans Singer, and—sans End!

XXIV

Alike for those who for To-DAY prepare,
And those that after a To-MORROW stare,
  A Muezzín from the Tower of Darkness cries,
"Fools! your Reward is neither Here nor There!"

XXV

Why, all the Saints and Sages who discuss'd
Of the Two Worlds so learnedly, are thrust
  Like foolish Prophets forth; their Words to Scorn
Are scatter'd, and their Mouths are stopt with Dust.

XXVI

Oh, come with old Khayyám, and leave the Wise
To talk; one thing is certain, that Life flies;
  One thing is certain, and the Rest is Lies;
The Flower that once has blown for ever dies.

XXVII

Myself when young did eagerly frequent
Doctor and Saint, and heard great Argument
  About it and about: but evermore
Came out by the same Door as in I went.

XXVIII

With them the Seed of Wisdom did I sow,
And with my own hand labour'd it to grow:
   And this was all the Harvest that I reap'd—
"I came like Water, and like Wind I go."

XXIX

Into this Universe, and *why* not knowing,
Nor *whence*, like Water willy-nilly flowing:
   And out of it, as Wind along the Waste,
I know not *whither*, willy-nilly blowing.

XXX

What, without asking, hither hurried *whence?*
And, without asking, *whither* hurried hence!
   Another and another Cup to drown
The Memory of this Impertinence!

XXXI

Up from Earth's Centre, through the Seventh Gate
I rose, and on the Throne of Saturn sate,
   And many Knots unravel'd by the Road;
But not the Knot of Human Death and Fate.

XXXII

There was a Door to which I found no Key:
There was a Veil past which I could not see:
   Some little Talk awhile of ME and THEE
There seemed—and then no more of THEE and ME.

XXXIII

Then to the rolling Heav'n itself I cried,
Asking, "What Lamp had Destiny to guide
   "Her little Children stumbling in the Dark?"
And—"A blind Understanding!" Heav'n replied.

24

XXXIV

Then to this earthen Bowl did I adjourn
My Lip the secret Well of Life to learn:
    And Lip to Lip it murmur'd—"While you live
"Drink!—for once dead you never shall return."

XXXV

I think the Vessel, that with fugitive
Articulation answer'd, once did live,
    And merry-make; and the cold Lip I kiss'd
How many Kisses might it take—and give!

XXXVI

For in the Market-place, one Dusk of Day,
I watch'd the Potter thumping his wet Clay:
    And with its all obliterated Tongue
It murmur'd—"Gently, Brother, gently, pray!"

XXXVII

Ah, fill the Cup:—what boots it to repeat
How Time is slipping underneath our Feet:
    Unborn To-morrow, and dead Yesterday,
Why fret about them if To-day be sweet!

XXXVIII

One Moment in Annihilation's Waste,
One Moment, of the Well of Life to taste—
    The Stars are setting and the Caravan
Starts for the Dawn of Nothing—Oh, make haste!

XXXIX

How long, how long, in infinite Pursuit
Of This and That endeavour and dispute?
    Better be merry with the fruitful Grape
Than sadden after none, or bitter, Fruit.

You know, my Friends, how long since in my House
For a new Marriage I did make Carouse:
   Divorced old barren Reason from my Bed,
And took the Daughter of the Vine to Spouse.

For "Is" and "Is-NOT" though *with* Rule and Line,
And "UP-AND-DOWN" *without*, I could define,
   I yet in all I only cared to know,
Was never deep in anything but—Wine.

And lately, by the Tavern Door agape,
Came stealing through the Dusk an Angel Shape
   Bearing a Vessel on his Shoulder; and
He bid me taste of it; and 'twas—the Grape!

The Grape that can with Logic absolute
The Two-and-Seventy jarring Sects confute:
   The subtle Alchemist that in a Trice
Life's leaden Metal into Gold transmute.

The mighty Mahmúd, the victorious Lord,
That all the misbelieving and black Horde
   Of Fears and Sorrows that infest the Soul
Scatters and slays with his enchanted Sword.

But leave the Wise to wrangle, and with me
The Quarrel of the Universe let be:
   And, in some corner of the Hubbub coucht,
Make Game of that which makes as much of Thee.

For in and out, above, about, below,
'Tis nothing but a Magic Shadow-show,
   Play'd in a Box whose Candle is the Sun,
Round which we Phantom Figures come and go.

And if the Wine you drink, the Lip you press,
End in the Nothing all Things end in—Yes—
   Then fancy while Thou art, Thou art but what
Thou shalt be—Nothing—Thou shalt not be less.

While the Rose blows along the River Brink,
With old Khayyám the Ruby Vintage drink:
   And when the Angel with his darker Draught
Draws up to Thee—take that, and do not shrink.

'Tis all a Chequer-board of Nights and Days
Where Destiny with Men for Pieces plays:
   Hither and thither moves, and mates, and slays,
And one by one back in the Closet lays.

The Ball no Question makes of Ayes and Noes,
But Right or Left as strikes the Player goes;
   And He that toss'd Thee down into the Field,
He knows about it all—HE knows—HE knows!

The Moving Finger writes; and, having writ,
Moves on: nor all thy Piety nor Wit
   Shall lure it back to cancel half a Line,
Nor all thy Tears wash out a Word of it.

LII

And that inverted Bowl we call The Sky,
Whereunder crawling coop't we live and die,
   Lift not thy hands to *It* for help—for It
Rolls impotently on as Thou or I.

LIII

With Earth's first Clay They did the Last Man's
      knead,
And then of the Last Harvest sow'd the Seed:
   Yea, the first Morning of Creation wrote
What the Last Dawn of Reckoning shall read.

LIV

I tell Thee this—When, starting from the Goal,
Over the shoulders of the flaming Foal
   Of Heav'n Parwín and Mushtara they flung,
In my predestin'd Plot of Dust and Soul

LV

The Vine had struck a Fibre; which about
If clings my Being—let the Súfi flout;
   Of my Base Metal may be filed a Key,
That shall unlock the Door he howls without.

LVI

And this I know: whether the one True Light,
Kindle to Love, or Wrathconsume me quite,
   One glimpse of It within the Tavern caught
Better than in the Temple lost outright.

LVII

Oh Thou, who didst with Pitfall and with Gin
Beset the Road I was to wander in,
   Thou wilt not with Predestination round
Enmesh me, and impute my Fall to Sin?

Oh, Thou, who Man of baser Earth didst make,
And who with Eden didst devise the Snake;
  For all the Sin wherewith the Face of Man
Is blacken'd, Man's Forgiveness give—and take!

*　　*　　*　　*

Kúza—Náma

Listen again. One Evening at the Close
Of Ramazán, ere the better Moon arose,
  In that old Potter's Shop I stood alone
With the clay Population round in Rows.

And, strange to tell, among that Earthen Lot
Some could articulate, while others not:
  And suddenly one more impatient cried—
"Who *is* the Potter, pray, and who the Pot?"

Then said another—"Surely not in vain
"My Substance from the common Earth was ta'en,
  "That He who subtly wrought me into Shape
"Should stamp me back to common Earth again."

Another said—"Why, ne'er a peevish Boy,
"Would break the Bowl from which he drank in Joy;
  "Shall He that *made* the Vessel in pure Love
"And Fansy, in an after Rage destroy!"

None answer'd this; but after Silence spake
A Vessel of a more ungainly Make:
  "They sneer at me for leaning all awry;
"What! did the Hand then of the Potter shake?"

LXIV

Said one—"Folks of a surly Tapster tell,
"And daub his Visage with the Smoke of Hell;
    "They talk of some strict Testing of us—Pish!
"He's a Good Fellow, and 'twill all be well."

LXV

Then said another with a long-drawn Sigh,
"My Clay with long oblivion is gone dry:
    "But, fill me with the old familiar Juice,
"Methinks I might recover by-and-bye!"

LXVI

So while the Vessels one by one were speaking,
One spied the little Crescent all were seeking:
    And then they jogg'd each other, "Brother!
        Brother!
"Hark to the Porter's Shoulder-knot a-creaking!"

*   *   *   *

LXVII

Ah, with the Grape my fading Life provide,
And wash my Body whence the Life has died,
    And in a Winding-sheet of Vine-leaf wrapt,
So bury me by some sweet Garden-side.

LXVIII

That ev'n my buried Ashes such a Snare
Of Perfume shall fling up into the Air,
    As not a True Believer passing by
But shall be overtaken unaware.

LXIX

Indeed the Idols I have loved so long
Have done my Credit in Men's Eye much wrong:
    Have drown'd my Honour in a shallow Cup,
And sold my Reputation for a Song.

Indeed, indeed, Repentance oft before
I swore—but was I sober when I swore?
   And then and then came Spring, and Rose-in-
      hand
My thread-bare Penitence apieces tore.

LXXI

And much as Wine has play'd the Infidel,
And robb'd me of my Robe of Honour—well,
   I often wonder what the Vintners buy
One half so precious as the Goods they sell.

LXXII

Alas, that Spring should vanish with the Rose!
That Youth's sweet-scented Manuscript should
      close!
   The Nightingale that in the Branches sang,
Ah, whence, and whither flown again, who knows!

LXXIII

Ah Love! could thou and I with Fate conspire
To grasp this sorry Scheme of Things entire,
   Would not we shatter it to bits—and then
Re-mould it nearer to the Heart's Desire!

LXXIV

Ah, Moon of my Delight who know'st no wane,
The Moon of Heav'n is rising once again:
   How oft hereafter rising shall she look
Through this same Garden after me—in vain!

LXXV

And when Thyself with shining Foot shall pass
Among the Guests Star-scatter'd on the Grass,
   And in thy joyous Errand reach the Spot
Where I made one—turn down an empty Glass!

TAMÁM SHUD.

TENNYSON, Alfred, Lord

ALFRED TENNYSON—1st baron Tennyson—(1809–1892) was born at Somersby, Lincolnshire. He was educated at Louth Grammar School, privately, and at Trinity College, Cambridge. He left the University disappointed and before taking a degree. By 1832, such poems as *The Lady of Shalott, The Lotos-Eaters* and *A Dream of Fair Women* had seen the light; by 1842, *Locksley Hall, Morte d'Arthur, Ulysses, The Vision of Sin, Break, break, break* and other work had been published. Popularity greeted the poet; a Civil List pension eased financial strain. *The Princess* appeared. Anonymously in 1850, Tennyson issued *In Memoriam*, seventeen years after the death of Arthur Hallam which occasioned it. That great poem established Tennyson's fame; and the Laureateship, vacant by Wordsworth's death, was bestowed on the poet. The Wellington *Ode, Maud, Idylls of the King, Enoch Arden*, the plays *Queen Mary* and *Harold, The Revenge*, the dramas *The Cup* and *Becket* and the poems *The Voyage of Maeldune, The Ancient Sage, Locksley Hall sixty years after* and *Crossing the Bar* may be singled out from his subsequent publications. He received, eight years before his death, a barony. He is buried in Westminster Abbey. Tennyson is in the very forefront of English poets. Praising or condemning the musical qualities of his verse, especially of his early writings, the critics have too often neglected to establish the poet's value as a mirror of contemporary thought. In Tennyson's writing is perfectly reflected the main philosophic speculations of the Victorian renascence.

The Lady of Shalott

PART I

On either side the water lie
Long fields of barley and of rye,
That clothe the wold and meet the sky;
And thro' the field the road runs by
      To many-tower'd Camelot;
And up and down the people go,
Gazing where the lilies blow
Round an island there below,
      The island of Shalott.

Willows whiten, aspens quiver,
Little breezes dusk and shiver
Thro' the wave that runs for ever
By the island in the river
   Flowing down to Camelot.
Four gray walls, and four gray towers,
Overlook a space of flowers,
And the silent isle imbowers
   The Lady of Shalott.

By the margin, willow-veil'd,
Slide the heavy barges trail'd
By slow horses; and unhail'd
The shallop flitteth silken-sail'd
   Skimming down to Camelot:
But who hath seen her wave her hand?
Or at the casement seen her stand?
Or is she known in all the land,
   The Lady of Shalott?

Only reapers, reaping early
In among the bearded barley,
Hear a song that echoes cheerly
From the river winding clearly,
   Down to tower'd Camelot:
And by the moon the reaper weary,
Piling sheaves in uplands airy,
Listening, whispers "'Tis the fairy
   Lady of Shalott."

PART II

There she weaves by night and day
A magic web with colours gay.
She has heard a whisper say,
A curse is on her if she stay
   To look down to Camelot.

She knows not what the curse may be,
And so she weaveth steadily,
And little other care hath she,
    The Lady of Shalott.

And moving thro' a mirror clear
That hangs before her all the year,
Shadows of the world appear.
There she sees the highway near
    Winding down to Camelot:
There the river eddy whirls,
And there the surly village-churls,
And the red cloaks of market girls,
    Pass onward from Shalott.

Sometimes a troop of damsels glad,
An abbot on an ambling pad,
Sometimes a curly shepherd-lad,
Or long-hair'd page in crimson clad,
    Goes by to tower'd Camelot;
And sometimes thro' the mirror blue
The knights come riding two and two:
She hath no loyal knight and true,
    The Lady of Shalott.

But in her web she still delights
To weave the mirror's magic sights,
For often thro' the silent nights
A funeral, with plumes and lights
    And music, went to Camelot:
Or when the moon was overhead,
Came two young lovers lately wed;
"I am half sick of shadows," said
    The Lady of Shalott.

PART III

A bow-shot from her bower-eaves,
He rode between the barley-sheaves,
The sun came dazzling thro' the leaves,
And flamed upon the brazen greaves
    Of bold Sir Lancelot.
A red-cross knight for ever kneel'd
To a lady in his shield,
That sparkled on the yellow field,
    Beside remote Shalott.

The gemmy bridle glitter'd free,
Like to some branch of stars we see
Hung in the golden Galaxy.
The bridle bells rang merrily
    As he rode down to Camelot:
And from his blazon'd baldric slung
A mighty silver bugle hung,
And as he rode his armour rung,
    Beside remote Shalott.

All in the blue unclouded weather
Thick-jewell'd shone the saddle-leather,
The helmet and the helmet-feather
Burn'd like one burning flame together,
    As he rode down to Camelot.
As often thro' the purple night,
Below the starry clusters bright,
Some bearded meteor, trailing light,
    Moves over still Shalott.

His broad clear brow in sunlight glow'd;
On burnish'd hooves his war-horse trode;
From underneath his helmet flow'd
His coal-black curls as on he rode,
    As he rode down to Camelot.
From the bank and from the river
He flash'd into the crystal mirror,
"Tirra lirra," by the river
    Sang Sir Lancelot.

She left the web, she left the loom,
She made three paces thro' the room,
She saw the water-lily bloom,
She saw the helmet and the plume,
    She look'd down to Camelot.
Out flew the web and floated wide;
The mirror crack'd from side to side;
"The curse is come upon me," cried
    The Lady of Shalott.

PART IV

In the stormy east-wind straining,
The pale yellow woods were waning,
The broad stream in his banks complaining,
Heavily the low sky raining
    Over tower'd Camelot;
Down she came and found a boat
Beneath a willow left afloat,
And round about the prow she wrote
    The Lady of Shalott.

And down the river's dim expanse
Like some bold seër in a trance,
Seeing all his own mischance—
With a glassy countenance
    Did she look to Camelot.
And at the closing of the day
She loosed the chain, and down she lay;
The broad stream bore her far away,
    The Lady of Shalott.

Lying, robed in snowy white
That loosely flew to left and right—
The leaves upon her falling light—
Thro' the noises of the night
    She floated down to Camelot:
And as the boat-head wound along
The willowy hills and fields among,
They heard her singing her last song,
    The Lady of Shalott.

Heard a carol, mournful, holy,
Chanted loudly, chanted lowly,
Till her blood was frozen slowly,
And her eyes were darken'd wholly,
  Turn'd to tower'd Camelot.
For ere she reach'd upon the tide
The first house by the water-side,
Singing in her song she died,
  The Lady of Shalott.

Under tower and balcony,
By garden-wall and gallery,
A gleaming shape she floated by,
Dead-pale between the houses high,
  Silent into Camelot.
Out upon the wharfs they came,
Knight and burgher, lord and dame,
And round the prow they read her name,
  The Lady of Shalott.

Who is this? and what is here?
And in the lighted palace near
Died the sound of royal cheer;
And they cross'd themselves for fear,
  All the knights at Camelot:
But Lancelot mused a little space;
He said, "She has a lovely face;
God in his mercy lend her grace,
  The Lady of Shalott."

The Lotos-Eaters: Choric Song

I

THERE is sweet music here that softer falls
Than petals from blown roses on the grass,
Or night-dews on still waters between walls
Of shadowy granite, in a gleaming pass;

Music that gentlier on the spirit lies,
Than tir'd eyelids upon tir'd eyes;
Music that brings sweet sleep down from the blissful
    skies.
Here are cool mosses deep,
And thro' the moss the ivies creep,
And in the stream the long-leaved flowers weep,
And from the craggy ledge the poppy hangs in sleep.

II

Why are we weigh'd upon with heaviness,
And utterly consumed with sharp distress,
While all things else have rest from weariness?
All things have rest: why should we toil alone,
We only toil, who are the first of things,
And make perpetual moan,
Still from one sorrow to another thrown:
Nor ever fold our wings,
And cease from wanderings,
Nor steep our brows in slumber's holy balm;
Nor harken what the inner spirit sings,
"There is no joy but calm!"
Why should we only toil, the roof and crown of
    things?

III

Lo! in the middle of the wood,
The folded leaf is woo'd from out the bud
With winds upon the branch, and there
Grows green and broad, and takes no care,
Sun-steep'd at noon, and in the moon
Nightly dew-fed; and turning yellow
Falls, and floats adown the air.
Lo! sweeten'd with the summer light,
The full-juiced apple, waxing over-mellow,
Drops in a silent autumn night.
All its allotted length of days,
The flower ripens in its place,

Ripens and fades, and falls, and hath no toil,
Fast-rooted in the fruitful soil.

IV

Hateful is the dark-blue sky,
Vaulted o'er the dark-blue sea.
Death is the end of life; ah, why
Should life all labour be?
Let us alone. Time driveth onward fast,
And in a little while our lips are dumb.
Let us alone. What is it that will last?
All things are taken from us, and become
Portions and parcels of the dreadful Past.
Let us alone. What pleasure can we have
To war with evil? Is there any peace
In ever climbing up the climbing wave?
All things have rest, and ripen toward the grave
In silence; ripen, fall and cease:
Give us long rest or death, dark death, or dreamful
      ease.

How sweet it were, hearing the downward stream,
With half-shut eyes ever to seem
Falling asleep in a half-dream!
To dream and dream, like yonder amber light,
Which will not leave the myrrh-bush on the height;
To hear each other's whisper'd speech;
Eating the Lotos day by day,
To watch the crisping ripples on the beach,
And tender curving lines of creamy spray;
To lend our hearts and spirits wholly
To the influence of mild-minded melancholy;
To muse and brood and live again in memory,
With those old faces of our infancy
Heap'd over with a mound of grass,
Two handfuls of white dust, shut in an urn of
      brass!

Dear is the memory of our wedded lives,
And dear the last embraces of our wives
And their warm tears: but all hath suffer'd change:
For surely now our household hearths are cold:
Our sons inherit us: our looks are strange:
And we should come like ghosts to trouble joy.
Or else the island princes over-bold
Have eat our substance, and the minstrel sings
Before them of the ten years' war in Troy,
And our great deeds, as half-forgotten things.
Is there confusion in the little isle?
Let what is broken so remain.
The Gods are hard to reconcile:
'Tis hard to settle order once again.
There *is* confusion worse than death,
Trouble on trouble, pain on pain,
Long labour unto aged breath,
Sore task to hearts worn out by many wars
And eyes grown dim with gazing on the pilot-stars.

VII

But, propt on beds of amaranth and moly,
How sweet (while warm airs lull us, blowing lowly)
With half-dropt eyelid still,
Beneath a heaven dark and holy,
To watch the long bright river drawing slowly
His waters from the purple hill—
To hear the dewy echoes calling
From cave to cave thro' the thick-twined vine—
To watch the emerald-colour'd water falling
Thro' many a wov'n acanthus-wreath divine!
Only to hear and see the far-off sparkling brine,
Only to hear were sweet, stretch'd out beneath the
      pine.

VIII

The Lotos blooms below the barren peak:
The Lotos blows by every winding creek:

All day the wind breathes low with mellower tone:
Thro' every hollow cave and alley lone
Round and round the spicy downs the yellow Lotos-
    dust is blown.
We have had enough of action, and of motion we,
Roll'd to starboard, roll'd to larboard, when the
    surge was seething free,
Where the wallowing monster spouted his foam-
    fountains in the sea.
Let us swear an oath, and keep it with an equal
    mind,
In the hollow Lotos-land to live and lie reclined
On the hills like Gods together, careless of man-
    kind.
For they lie beside their nectar, and the bolts are
    hurl'd
Far below them in the valleys, and the clouds are
    lightly curl'd
Round their golden houses, girdled with the gleam-
    ing world:
Where they smile in secret, looking over wasted
    lands,
Blight and famine, plague and earthquake, roaring
    deeps and fiery sands,
Clanging fights, and flaming towns, and sinking
    ships, and praying hands.
But they smile, they find a music centred in a
    doleful song
Steaming up, a lamentation and an ancient tale of
    wrong,
Like a tale of little meaning tho' the words are
    strong;
Chanted from an ill-used race of men that cleave
    the soil,
Sow the seed, and reap the harvest with enduring
    toil,
Storing yearly little dues of wheat, and wine and
    oil;

Till they perish and they suffer—some, 'tis whis-
    per'd—down in hell
Suffer endless anguish, others in Elysian valleys
    dwell,
Resting weary limbs at last on beds of asphodel.
Surely, surely, slumber is more sweet than toil, the
    shore
Than labour in the deep mid-ocean, wind and wave
    and oar;
Oh rest ye, brother mariners, we will not wander
    more.

Ulysses

IT little profits that an idle king,
By this still hearth, among these barren crags,
Match'd with an aged wife, I mete and dole
Unequal laws unto a savage race,
That hoard, and sleep, and feed, and know not me.
I cannot rest from travel: I will drink
Life to the lees: all times I have enjoy'd
Greatly, have suffer'd greatly, both with those
That loved me, and alone; on shore, and when
Thro' scudding drifts the rainy Hyades
Vext the dim sea: I am become a name;
For always roaming with a hungry heart
Much have I seen and known; cities of men
And manners, climates, councils, governments,
Myself not least, but honour'd of them all;
And drunk delight of battle with my peers,
Far on the ringing plains of windy Troy.
I am a part of all that I have met;
Yet all experience is an arch wherethro'
Gleams that untravell'd world, whose margin fades
For ever and for ever when I move.
How dull it is to pause, to make an end,
To rust unburnish'd, not to shine in use!
As tho' to breathe were life. Life piled on life
Were all too little, and of one to me

Little remains: but every hour is saved
From that eternal silence, something more,
A bringer of new things; and vile it were
For some three suns to store and hoard myself,
And this gray spirit yearning in desire
To follow knowledge like a sinking star,
Beyond the utmost bound of human thought.
 This is my son, mine own Telemachus,
To whom I leave the sceptre and the isle—
Well-loved of me, discerning to fulfil
This labour, by slow prudence to make mild
A rugged people, and thro' soft degrees
Subdue them to the useful and the good.
Most blameless is he, centred in the sphere
Of common duties, decent not to fail
In offices of tenderness, and pay
Meet adoration to my household gods,
When I am gone. He works his work, I mine.
 There lies the port; the vessel puffs her sail:
There gloom the dark broad seas. My mariners,
Souls that have toil'd, and wrought, and thought
  with me—
That ever with a frolic welcome took
The thunder and the sunshine, and opposed
Free hearts, free foreheads—you and I are old;
Old age hath yet his honour and his toil;
Death closes all: but something ere the end,
Some work of noble note, may yet be done,
Not unbecoming men that strove with Gods.
The lights begin to twinkle from the rocks:
The long day wanes: the slow moon climbs: the
  deep
Moans round with many voices. Come, my friends,
'Tis not too late to seek a newer world.
Push off, and sitting well in order smite
The sounding furrows; for my purpose holds
To sail beyond the sunset, and the baths
Of all the western stars, until I die.

It may be that the gulfs will wash us down:
It may be we shall touch the Happy Isles,
And see the great Achilles, whom we knew.
Tho' much is taken, much abides; and tho'
We are not now that strength which in old days
Moved earth and heaven; that which we are, we are;
One equal temper of heroic hearts,
Made weak by time and fate, but strong in will
To strive, to seek, to find, and not to yield.

Break, Break, Break

BREAK, break, break,
   On thy cold gray stones, O Sea!
And I would that my tongue could utter
   The thoughts that arise in me.

O well for the fisherman's boy,
   That he shouts with his sister at play!
O well for the sailor lad,
   That he sings in his boat on the bay!

And the stately ships go on
   To their haven under the hill;
But O for the touch of a vanish'd hand,
   And the sound of a voice that is still!

Break, break, break,
   At the foot of thy crags, O Sea!
But the tender grace of a day that is dead
   Will never come back to me.

From *The Princess*

"TEARS, idle tears, I know not what they mean,
Tears from the depth of some divine despair
Rise in the heart, and gather to the eyes,
In looking on the happy Autumn-fields,
And thinking of the days that are no more.

"Fresh as the first beam glittering on a sail,
That brings our friends up from the underworld,
Sad as the last which reddens over one
That sinks with all we love below the verge;
So sad, so fresh, the days that are no more.

"Ah, sad and strange as in dark summer dawns
The earliest pipe of half-awaken'd birds
To dying ears, when unto dying eyes
The casement slowly grows a glimmering square;
So sad, so strange, the days that are no more.

"Dear as remember'd kisses after death,
And sweet as those by hopeless fancy feign'd
On lips that are for others; deep as love,
Deep as first love, and wild with all regret;
O Death in Life, the days that are no more."

"Now sleeps the crimson petal, now the white;
Nor waves the cypress in the palace walk;
Nor winks the gold fin in the porphyry font:
The fire-fly wakens: waken thou with me.

Now droops the milkwhite peacock like a ghost,
And like a ghost she glimmers on to me.

Now lies the Earth all Danaë to the stars,
And all thy heart lies open unto me.

Now slides the silent meteor on, and leaves
A shining furrow, as thy thoughts in me.

Now folds the lily all her sweetness up,
And slips into the bosom of the lake:
So fold thyself, my dearest, thou, and slip
Into my bosom and be lost in me."

From *In Memoriam*

THE wish, that of the living whole
    No life may fail beyond the grave,
    Derives it not from what we have
The likest God within the soul?

Are God and Nature then at strife,
    That Nature lends such evil dreams?
    So careful of the type she seems,
So careless of the single life;

       *   *   *   *

"So careful of the type?" but no.
    From scarped cliff and quarried stone
    She cries, "A thousand types are gone:
I care for nothing, all shall go.

"Thou makest thine appeal to me:
    I bring to life, I bring to death:
    The spirit does but mean the breath:
I know no more." And he, shall he,

Man, her last work, who seem'd so fair,
    Such splendid purpose in his eyes,
    Who roll'd the psalm to wintry skies,
Who built him fanes of fruitless prayer,

Who trusted God was love indeed
    And love Creation's final law—
    Tho' Nature, red in tooth and claw
With ravine, shriek'd against his creed—

Who loved, who suffer'd countless ills,
    Who battled for the True, the Just,
    Be blown about the desert dust,
Or seal'd within the iron hills?

No more? A monster then, a dream,
    A discord. Dragons of the prime,
    That tare each other in their slime,
Were mellow music match'd with him.

O life as futile, then, as frail!
    O for thy voice to soothe and bless!
    What hope of answer, or redress?
Behind the veil, behind the veil.

From *The Ancient Sage*

A THOUSAND summers ere the time of Christ
From out his ancient city came a Seer
Whom one that loved, and honour'd him, and yet
Was no disciple, richly garb'd, but worn
From wasteful living, follow'd—in his hand
A scroll of verse—till that old man before
A cavern whence an affluent fountain pour'd
From darkness into daylight, turn'd and spoke.

*   *   *   *

Thou canst not prove the Nameless, O my son,
Nor canst thou prove the world thou movest in,
Thou canst not prove that thou art body alone,
Nor canst thou prove that thou art spirit alone,
Nor canst thou prove that thou art both in one:
Thou canst not prove thou art immortal, no
Nor yet that thou art mortal—nay my son,
Thou canst not prove that I, who speak with thee,
Am not thyself in converse with thyself,
For nothing worthy proving can be proven,
Nor yet disproven: wherefore thou be wise,
Cleave ever to the sunnier side of doubt,
And cling to Faith beyond the forms of Faith!
She reels not in the storm of warring words,
She brightens at the clash of "Yes" and "No",
She sees the Best that glimmers thro' the Worst,
She feels the Sun is hid but for a night,

She spies the summer thro' the winter bud,
She tastes the fruit before the blossom falls,
She hears the lark within the songless egg,
She finds the fountain where they wail'd "Mirage"!

*　　*　　*　　*

Let be thy wail and help thy fellow men,
And make thy gold thy vassal not thy king,
And fling free alms into the beggar's bowl,
And send the day into the darken'd heart;
Nor list for guerdon in the voice of men,
A dying echo from a falling wall;
Nor care—for Hunger hath the Evil eye—
To vex the noon with fiery gems, or fold
Thy presence in the silk of sumptuous looms;
Nor roll thy viands on a luscious tongue,
Nor drown thyself with flies in honied wine;
Nor thou be rageful, like a handled bee,
And lose thy life by usage of thy sting;
Nor harm an adder thro' the lust for harm,
Nor make a snail's horn shrink for wantonness;
And more—think well! Do-well will follow thought,
And in the fatal sequence of this world
An evil thought may soil thy children's blood;
But curb the beast would cast thee in the mire,
And leave the hot swamp of voluptuousness
A cloud between the Nameless and thyself,
And lay thine uphill shoulder to the wheel,
And climb the Mount of Blessing, whence, if thou
Look higher, then—perchance—thou mayest—
         beyond
A hundred ever-rising mountain lines,
And past the range of Night and Shadow—see
The high-heaven dawn of more than mortal day
Strike on the Mount of Vision!
                              So, farewell.

Crossing the Bar

SUNSET and evening star,
  And one clear call for me!
And may there be no moaning of the bar,
  When I put out to sea,

But such a tide as moving seems asleep,
  Too full for sound and foam,
When that which drew from out the boundless deep
  Turns again home.

Twilight and evening bell,
  And after that the dark!
And may there be no sadness of farewell,
  When I embark;

For tho' from out our bourne of Time and Place
  The flood may bear me far,
I hope to see my Pilot face to face
  When I have crost the bar.

HOLMES, Oliver Wendell

OLIVER WENDELL HOLMES (1809–1894), born at Cambridge, Massachusetts, graduated at Harvard, specialised in medicine, travelled in Europe and professed Anatomy successively at Dartmouth and Harvard. *The Autocrat of the Breakfast Table* brought him a fame to which *The Professor at the Breakfast Table*, subsequent prose and scattered verse added.

The Chambered Nautilus

THIS is the ship of pearl, which, poets feign,
    Sails the unshadowed main,—
    The venturous bark that flings
On the sweet summer wind its purpled wings
In gulfs enchanted, where the Siren sings,
    And coral reefs lie bare,
Where the cold sea-maids rise to sun their stream-
    ing hair.

Its webs of living gauze no more unfurl;
>>Wrecked is the ship of pearl!
>>And every chambered cell,
Where its dim dreaming life was wont to dwell,
As the frail tenant shaped his growing shell,
>>Before thee lies revealed,—
Its irised ceiling rent, its sunless crypt unsealed!

Year after year beheld the silent toil
>>That spread his lustrous coil;
>>Still, as the spiral grew,
He left the past year's dwelling for the new,
Stole with soft step its shining archway through,
>>Built up its idle door,
Stretched in his last-found home, and knew the old
>>>no more.

Thanks for the heavenly message brought by thee,
>>Child of the wandering sea,
>>Cast from her lap, forlorn!
From thy dead lips a clearer note is born
Than ever Triton blew from wreathéd horn!
>>While on mine ear it rings,
Through the deep caves of thought I hear a voice
>>>that sings:—

Build thee more stately mansions, O my soul,
>>As the swift seasons roll!
>>Leave thy low-vaulted past!
Let each new temple, nobler than the last,
Shut thee from heaven with a dome more vast,
>>Till thou at length art free,
Leaving thine outgrown shell by life's unresting
>>>sea!

BROWNING, Robert

ROBERT BROWNING (1812–1889), born in London, was schooled in Peckham and by a private tutor; he then studied at University College, London. From 1832 to 1834 *Pauline, Porphyria's Lover* and *Johannes Agricola* were written. *Paracelsus*, the play *Strafford* and *Sordello* "tightly compressed and abstrusely dark" followed. The first volume of the series to which Browning gave the title *Bells and Pomegranates* appeared in 1841. That was the play *Pippa Passes. King Victor and King Charles*, a play, *Dramatic Lyrics*, the three plays *The Return of the Druses, A Blot in the 'Scutcheon, Colombe's Birthday, Dramatic Romances and Lyrics*, the plays *Luria* and *A Soul's Tragedy* completed, by 1846, the plan. Browning's marriage to Elizabeth Barrett took place in 1846. Most of the next fifteen years (till his wife's death, 1861) were spent abroad. The period was unproductive; but, in 1855, Browning issued *Men and Women. Dramatis Personæ* and the long, elaborate murder story *The Ring and the Book* are his outstanding later work. He was buried in Westminster Abbey. In Browning packed thought spills over; but, though his expression is rugged, his versification is far from unworkmanlike. The poet's optimism is pronounced. He is unapproachable as a writer of dramatic monologue. When it is recognised that he usually means quite literally what he says, Browning becomes easier to read. Yet the mental effort required for the perusal of his longer work will probably determine that this writer's fame will rest upon the shorter 1832–34 pieces, on the *Pied Piper of Hamelin* (*Dramatic Lyrics*), *The Lost Leader, Home-Thoughts from Abroad, The Confessional* (*Dramatic Romances and Lyrics*) and upon such work as *Fra Lippo Lippi, Master Hugues of Saxe-Gotha, Bishop Blougram's Apology, Andrea del Sarto, A Grammarian's Funeral* (*Men and Women*) and *Prospice*—a late fragment.

Johannes Agricola in Meditation

THERE'S heaven above, and night by night
   I look right through its gorgeous roof;
No suns and moons though e'er so bright
   Avail to stop me; splendour-proof
   I keep the broods of stars aloof:

For I intend to get to God,
　For 'tis to God I speed so fast,
For in God's breast, my own abode,
　Those shoals of dazzling glory, passed,
　I lay my spirit down at last.
I lie where I have always lain,
　God smiles as he has always smiled;
Ere suns and moons could wax and wane,
　Ere stars were thundergirt, or piled
　The heavens, God thought on me his child;
Ordained a life for me, arrayed
　Its circumstances every one
To the minutest; ay, God said
　This head this hand should rest upon
　Thus, ere he fashioned star or sun.
And having thus created me,
　Thus rooted me, he bade me grow,
Guiltless for ever, like a tree
　That buds and blooms, nor seeks to know
　The law by which it prospers so:
But sure that thought and word and deed
　All go to swell his love for me,
Me, made because that love had need
　Of something irreversibly
　Pledged solely its content to be.
Yes, yes, a tree which must ascend,
　No poison-gourd foredoomed to stoop!
I have God's warrant, could I blend
　All hideous sins, as in a cup,
　To drink the mingled venoms up;
Secure my nature will convert
　The draught to blossoming gladness fast:
While sweet dews turn to the gourd's hurt,
　And bloat, and while they bloat it, blast,
　As from the first its lot was cast.
For as I lie, smiled on, full-fed
　By unexhausted power to bless,
I gaze below on hell's fierce bed,

And those its waves of flame oppress,
  Swarming in ghastly wretchedness;
Whose life on earth aspired to be
  One altar-smoke, so pure!—to win
If not love like God's love to me,
  At least to keep his anger in;
  And all their striving turned to sin.
Priest, doctor, hermit, monk grown white
  With prayer, the broken-hearted nun,
The martyr, the wan acolyte,
  The incense-swinging child,—undone
  Before God fashioned star or sun!
God, whom I praise; how could I praise,
  If such as I might understand,
Make out and reckon on his ways,
  And bargain for his love, and stand,
  Paying a price, at his right hand?

From *Pippa Passes*

THE year's at the spring,
And day's at the morn;
Morning's at seven;
The hill-side's dew-pearled;
The lark's on the wing;
The snail's on the thorn:
God's in his heaven—
All's right with the world!

The Lost Leader

I

JUST for a handful of silver he left us,
  Just for a riband to stick in his coat—
Found the one gift of which fortune bereft us,
  Lost all the others she lets us devote;
They, with the gold to give, doled him out silver,
  So much was theirs who so little allowed:
How all our copper had gone for his service!

Rags—were they purple, his heart had been
   proud!
We that had loved him so, followed him, honoured
   him,
   Lived in his mild and magnificent eye,
Learned his great language, caught his clear accents,
   Made him our pattern to live and to die!
Shakespeare was of us, Milton was for us,
   Burns, Shelley, were with us,—they watch from
      their graves!
He alone breaks from the van and the freemen,
   —He alone sinks to the rear and the slaves!

II

We shall march prospering,—not thro' his presence;
   Songs may inspirit us,—not from his lyre;
Deeds will be done,—while he boasts his quiescence,
   Still bidding crouch whom the rest bade aspire:
Blot out his name, then, record one lost soul more,
   One task more declined, one more footpath untrod,
One more devils'-triumph and sorrow for angels,
   One wrong more to man, one more insult to God!
Life's night begins: let him never come back to us!
   There would be doubt, hesitation and pain,
Forced praise on our part—the glimmer of twilight,
   Never glad confident morning again!
Best fight on well, for we taught him—strike
   gallantly,
   Menace our heart ere we master his own;
Then let him receive the new knowledge and wait us,
   Pardoned in heaven, the first by the throne!

From *Home-Thoughts from Abroad*

I

Oh, to be in England
Now that April's there,
And whoever wakes in England
Sees, some morning, unaware,

54

That the lowest boughs and the brushwood sheaf
Round the elm-tree bole are in tiny leaf,
While the chaffinch sings on the orchard bough
In England—now!

II

And after April, when May follows,
And the whitethroat builds, and all the swallows!
Hark, where my blossomed pear-tree in the hedge
Leans to the field and scatters on the clover
Blossoms and dewdrops—at the bent spray's edge—
That's the wise thrush; he sings each song twice
      over,
Lest you should think he never could recapture
The first fine careless rapture!
And though the fields look rough with hoary dew,
All will be gay when noontide wakes anew
The buttercups, the little children's dower
—Far brighter than this gaudy melon-flower!

From *Fra Lippo Lippi*

Flower o' the rose,
If I've been merry, what matter who knows?
And so as I was stealing back again
To get to bed and have a bit of sleep
Ere I rise up to-morrow and go work
On Jerome knocking at his poor old breast
With his great round stone to subdue the flesh,
You snap me of the sudden. Ah, I see!
Though your eye twinkles still, you shake your
      head—
Mine's shaved,—a monk, you say—the sting's in
      that!
If Master Cosimo announced himself,
Mum's the word naturally; but a monk!
Come, what am I a beast for? tell us, now!
I was a baby when my mother died
And father died and left me in the street.

I starved there, God knows how, a year or two
On fig-skins, melon-parings, rinds and shucks,
Refuse and rubbish. One fine frosty day,
My stomach being empty as your hat,
The wind doubled me up and down I went.
Old Aunt Lapaccia trussed me with one hand,
(Its fellow was a stinger as I knew)
And so along the wall, over the bridge,
By the straight cut to the convent. Six words there,
While I stood munching my first bread that month:
"So, boy, you're minded," quoth the good fat father
Wiping his own mouth, 'twas refection-time—
"To quit this very miserable world?
Will you renounce"..."the mouthful of bread?"
        thought I;
By no means! Brief, they made a monk of me;
I did renounce the world, its pride and greed,
Palace, farm, villa, shop and banking-house,
Trash, such as these poor devils of Medici
Have given their hearts to—all at eight years old.
Well, sir, I found in time, you may be sure,
'Twas not for nothing—the good bellyful,
The warm serge and the rope that goes all round,
And day-long blessed idleness beside!
"Let's see what the urchin's fit for"—that came next.
Not overmuch their way, I must confess.
Such a to-do! They tried me with their books.
Lord, they'd have taught me Latin in pure waste!
Flower o' the clove,
All the Latin I construe is, "amo" I love!
But, mind you, when a boy starves in the streets
Eight years together, as my fortune was,
Watching folk's faces to know who will fling
The bit of half-stripped grape-bunch he desires,
And who will curse or kick him for his pains,—
Which gentleman processional and fine,
Holding a candle to the Sacrament,
Will wink and let him lift a plate and catch

The droppings of the wax to sell again,
Or holla for the Eight and have him whipped,—
How say I?—nay, which dog bites, which lets drop
His bone from the heap of offal in the street,—
Why, soul and sense of him grow sharp alike,
He learns the look of things, and none the less
For admonitions from the hunger-pinch.
I had a store of such remarks, be sure,
Which, after I found leisure, turned to use.
I drew men's faces on my copy-books,
Scrawled them within the antiphonary's marge,
Joined legs and arms to the long music-notes,
Found nose and eyes and chin for A's and B's,
And made a string of pictures of the world
Betwixt the ins and outs of verb and noun,
On the wall, the bench, the door. The monks looked
      black.
"Nay," quoth the Prior, "turn him out, d'ye say?
In no wise. Lose a crow and catch a lark.
What if at last we get our man of parts,
We Carmelites, like those Camaldolese
And Preaching Friars, to do our church up fine
And put the front on it that ought to be!"
And hereupon they bade me daub away.
Thank you! my head being crammed, the walls a
      blank,
Never was such prompt disemburdening.
First, every sort of monk, the black and white,
I drew them, fat and lean: then, folks at church,
From good old gossips waiting to confess
Their cribs of barrel-droppings, candle-ends,—
To the breathless fellow at the altar-foot,
Fresh from his murder, safe and sitting there
With the little children round him in a row
Of admiration, half for his beard and half
For that white anger of his victim's son
Shaking a fist at him with one fierce arm,
Signing himself with the other because of Christ

(Whose sad face on the cross sees only this
After the passion of a thousand years)
Till some poor girl, her apron o'er her head
(Which the intense eyes looked through) came at eve
On tip-toe, said a word, dropped in a loaf,
Her pair of ear-rings and a bunch of flowers
(The brute took growling), prayed, and then was
        gone.
I painted all, then cried " 'Tis ask and have;
Choose, for more's ready!"—laid the ladder flat,
And showed my covered bit of cloister-wall.

      *   *   *   *

The Prior and the learned pulled a face
And stopped all that in no time. "How? what's here?
Quite from the mark of painting, bless us all!
Faces, arms, legs and bodies like the true
As much as pea and pea! it's devil's-game!
Your business is not to catch men with show,
With homage to the perishable clay,
But lift them over it, ignore it all,
Make them forget there's such a thing as flesh.
Your business is to paint the souls of men—
Man's soul, and it's a fire, smoke...no it's not...
It's vapour done up like a new-born babe—
(In that shape when you die it leaves your mouth)
It's...well, what matters talking, it's the soul!
Give us no more of body than shows soul!
Here's Giotto, with his Saint a-praising God,
That sets us praising,—why not stop with him?
Why put all thoughts of praise out of our heads
With wonder at lines, colours, and what not?
Paint the soul, never mind the legs and arms!
Rub all out, try at it a second time."

      *   *   *   *

"Rub all out!" Well, well, there's my life, in short,
And so the thing has gone on ever since.
I'm grown a man no doubt, I've broken bounds:

You should not take a fellow eight years old
And make him swear to never kiss the girls.
     *   *   *   *
For me, I think I speak as I was taught—
I always see the garden and God there
A-making man's wife—and, my lesson learned,
The value and significance of flesh,
I can't unlearn ten minutes afterwards.

  'You understand me: I'm a beast, I know.
But see, now—why, I see as certainly
As that the morning-star's about to shine,
What will hap some day. We've a youngster here
Comes to our convent, studies what I do,
Slouches and stares and lets no atom drop:
His name is Guidi—he'll not mind the monks—
They call him Hulking Tom, he lets them talk—
He picks my practice up—he'll paint apace,
I hope so—though I never live so long,
I know what's sure to follow. You be judge!
You speak no Latin more than I, belike;
However, you're my man, you've seen the world
—The beauty and the wonder and the power,
The shapes of things, their colours, lights and shades,
Changes, surprises,—and God made it all!
—For what? Do you feel thankful, ay or no,
For this fair town's face, yonder river's line,
The mountain round it and the sky above,
Much more the figures of man, woman, child,
These are the frame to? What's it all about?
To be passed over, despised? or dwelt upon,
Wondered at? oh, this last of course!—you say.
But why not do as well as say,—paint these
Just as they are, careless what comes of it?
God's works—paint anyone, and count it crime
To let a truth slip. Don't object, "His works
Are here already; nature is complete:
Suppose you reproduce her—(which you can't)
There's no advantage! you must beat her, then."

For, don't you mark? we're made so that we love
   First when we see them painted, things we have
        passed
Perhaps a hundred times nor cared to see;
And so they are better, painted—better to us,
Which is the same thing. Art was given for that.

Prospice

FEAR death?—to feel the fog in my throat,
   The mist in my face,
When the snows begin, and the blasts denote
   I am nearing the place,
The power of the night, the press of the storm,
   The post of the foe;
Where he stands, the Arch Fear in a visible form,
   Yet the strong man must go:
For the journey is done and the summit attained,
   And the barriers fall,
Though a battle's to fight ere the guerdon be gained,
   The reward of it all.
I was ever a fighter, so—one fight more,
   The best and the last!
I would hate that death bandaged my eyes, and
        forbore,
   And bade me creep past.
No! let me taste the whole of it, fare like my peers
   The heroes of old,
Bear the brunt, in a minute pay glad life's arrears
   Of pain, darkness and cold.
For sudden the worst turns the best to the brave,
   The black minute's at end,
And the elements' rage, the fiend-voices that rave,
   Shall dwindle, shall blend,
Shall change, shall become first a peace out of pain,
   Then a light, then thy breast,
O thou soul of my soul! I shall clasp thee again,
   And with God be the rest!

BRONTË, Emily

EMILY BRONTË (1818–1848) was born at Thornton, near Bradford, of Celtic parentage. Within two years of her birth her father became incumbent of Haworth on the Yorkshire moorlands. Emily was taught at home, at private schools and, for a short time, in Brussels. The Yorkshire moorlands moulded her. She was associated with her sisters Charlotte and Anne in the production of the poems of "Currer, Ellis and Acton Bell." Her novel *Wuthering Heights*, which "hung fire," is now recognised as one of the masterpieces of the language. Only with the work of Thomas Hardy is her writing, prose or verse, all too small in quantity, comparable.

No coward soul is mine,
No trembler in the world's storm-troubled sphere:
I see Heaven's glories shine,
And faith shines equal, arming me from fear.

O God within my breast,
Almighty, ever-present Deity!
Life—that in me has rest,
As I—undying Life—have power in Thee!

Vain are the thousand creeds
That move men's hearts: unutterably vain;
Worthless as withered weeds,
Or idlest froth amid the boundless main,

To waken doubt in one
Holding so fast by Thine infinity;
So surely anchored on
The steadfast rock of immortality.

With wide-embracing love
Thy Spirit animates eternal years,
Pervades and broods above,
Changes, sustains, dissolves, creates, and rears.

Though earth and man were gone,
And suns and universes ceased to be,
And Thou were left alone,
Every existence would exist in Thee.

There is not room for Death,
Nor atom that his might could render void:
Thou—Thou art Being and Breath,
And what Thou art may never be destroyed.

CLOUGH, Arthur Hugh

Arthur Hugh Clough (1819–1861) was born in Liverpool, of Welsh-Yorkshire parentage, and educated in Chester, at Rugby and at Balliol College, Oxford. He resigned a fellowship of Oriel College, Oxford, on the ground that retention implied approval of the XXXIX Articles. After a sojourn in America he settled as an official of the education department of the Privy Council. The clever hexameters of *The Bothie of Tober-na-Vuolich* secured him a certain amount of attention; but his reputation is likely to rest upon *Jacob's Wives*, *The Shadow*, *Easter Day*, full of satire against organised Christianity, the curious dramatic poem *Dipsychus* (a sort of *Faust*) and *Say not, the struggle nought availeth*. He is buried in Florence.

Say not, the struggle nought availeth,
The labour and the wounds are vain,
The enemy faints not, nor faileth,
And as things have been they remain.

If hopes were dupes, fears may be liars;
It may be, in yon smoke concealed,
Your comrades chase e'en now the fliers,
And, but for you, possess the field.

For while the tired waves, vainly breaking,
Seem here no painful inch to gain,
Far back, through creeks and inlets making,
Comes silent, flooding in, the main.

And not by eastern windows only,
    When daylight comes, comes in the light;
In front, the sun climbs slow, how slowly,
    But westward, look, the land is bright.

KINGSLEY, Charles

CHARLES KINGSLEY (1819–1875) was born at Holne,
Devon. He attended a school at Clifton and Helston
Grammar School; afterwards he studied at King's College, London, and Magdalene College, Cambridge.
Taking Anglican orders, he joined with Maurice and
others to advocate "Christian Socialism"—which was far
from radical. Novels—*Yeast* (containing the striking
poem, *The Poacher's Widow*), *Alton Locke*, *Hypatia* and
Westward Ho!—appeared. Kingsley later entered upon
the controversy which drew from Newman the *Apologia*.
Kingsley's poetry possesses genuine merits; usually it is
vigorous.

Airly Beacon

AIRLY Beacon, Airly Beacon;
    Oh the pleasant sight to see
Shires and towns from Airly Beacon,
    While my love climbed up to me!

Airly Beacon, Airly Beacon;
    Oh the happy hours we lay
Deep in fern on Airly Beacon,
    Courting through the summer's day!

Airly Beacon, Airly Beacon;
    Oh the weary haunt for me,
All alone on Airly Beacon,
    With his baby on my knee!

Ode to the North-East Wind

Welcome, wild North-easter!
    Shame it is to see
Odes to every zephyr;
    Ne'er a verse to thee.

Welcome, black North-easter!
  O'er the German foam;
O'er the Danish moorlands,
  From thy frozen home.
Tired we are of summer,
  Tired of gaudy glare,
Showers soft and steaming,
  Hot and breathless air.
Tired of listless dreaming,
  Through the lazy day:
Jovial wind of winter,
  Turn us out to play!
Sweep the golden reed-beds;
  Crisp the lazy dyke;
Hunger into madness
  Every plunging pike.
Fill the lake with wild-fowl;
  Fill the marsh with snipe;
While on dreary moorlands
  Lonely curlew pipe.
Through the black fir-forest
  Thunder harsh and dry,
Shattering down the snow-flakes
  Off the curdled sky.
Hark! The brave North-easter!
  Breast-high lies the scent,
On by holt and headland,
  Over heath and bent.
Chime, ye dappled darlings,
  Through the sleet and snow.
Who can over-ride you?
  Let the horses go!
Chime, ye dappled darlings,
  Down the roaring blast;
You shall see a fox die
  Ere an hour be past.
Go! and rest to-morrow,
  Hunting in your dreams,

While our skates are ringing
  O'er the frozen streams.
Let the luscious South-wind
  Breathe in lovers' sighs,
While the lazy gallants
  Bask in ladies' eyes.
What does he but soften
  Heart alike and pen?
'Tis the hard grey weather
  Breeds hard English men.
What's the soft South-wester?
  'Tis the ladies' breeze,
Bringing home their true loves
  Out of all the seas:
But the black North-easter,
  Through the snowstorm hurled,
Drives our English hearts of oak
  Seaward round the world.
Come, as came our fathers,
  Heralded by thee,
Conquering from the eastward,
  Lords by land and sea.
Come; and strong within us
  Stir the Vikings' blood;
Bracing brain and sinew;
  Blow, thou wind of God!

INGELOW, Jean

Jean Ingelow (1820–1897) was born at Boston, Lincoln-shire. The following poem appeared in 1863.

The High Tide on the Coast of Lincolnshire (1571)

The old mayor climbed the belfry tower,
  The ringers ran by two, by three;
"Pull, if ye never pulled before;
  Good ringers, pull your best," quoth he.

"Play uppe, play uppe, O Boston bells!
Ply all your changes, all your swells,
    Play uppe *The Brides of Enderby*."

Men say it was a stolen tyde—
    The Lord that sent it, He knows all;
But in myne ears doth still abide
    The message that the bells let fall:
And there was naught of strange, beside
The flight of mews and peewits pied
    By millions crouched on the old sea wall.

I sat and spun within the doore,
    My thread brake off, I raised myne eyes;
The level sun, like ruddy ore,
    Lay sinking in the barren skies;
And dark against day's golden death
She moved where Lindis wandereth,
My sonne's faire wife, Elizabeth.

"Cusha! Cusha! Cusha!" calling,
Ere the early dews were falling,
Farre away I heard her song.
"Cusha! Cusha!" all along;
Where the reedy Lindis floweth,
    Floweth, floweth,
From the meads where melick groweth
Faintly came her milking song.—

"Cusha! Cusha! Cusha!" calling,
"For the dews will soone be falling;
Leave your meadow grasses mellow,
    Mellow, mellow;
Quit your cowslips, cowslips yellow;
Come uppe Whitefoot, come uppe Lightfoot;
Quit the stalks of parsley hollow,
    Hollow, hollow;
Come uppe Jetty, rise and follow,
From the clovers lift your head;

66

Come uppe Whitefoot, come uppe Lightfoot,
Come uppe Jetty, rise and follow,
Jetty, to the milking shed."

If it be long, aye, long ago,
  When I beginne to think howe long,
Againe I hear the Lindis flow,
  Swift as an arrowe, sharp and strong;
And all the aire it seemeth mee
Bin full of floating bells (sayth shee),
That ring the tune of *Enderby*.

Alle fresh the level pasture lay,
  And not a shadowe mote be seene,
Save where full fyve good miles away
  The steeple towered from out the greene;
And lo! the great bell farre and wide
Was heard in all the country side
That Saturday at eventide.

The swannerds where their sedges are
  Moved on in sunset's golden breath,
The shepherde lads I heard afarre,
  And my sonne's wife, Elizabeth;
Till floating o'er the grassy sea
Came downe that kyndly message free,
The *Brides of Mavis Enderby*.

Then some looked uppe into the sky,
  And all along where Lindis flows
To where the goodly vessels lie,
  And where the lordly steeple shows.
They sayde, "And why should this thing be?
What danger lowers by land or sea?
They ring the tune of *Enderby*!

For evil news from Mablethorpe,
  Of pyrate galleys warping down;
For shippes ashore beyond the scorpe,
  They have not spared to wake the towne:

But while the west bin red to see,
And storms be none, and pyrates flee,
Why ring *The Brides of Enderby?*"

I looked without, and lo! my sonne
   Came riding downe with might and main:
He raised a shout as he drew on,
   Till all the welkin rang again,
"Elizabeth! Elizabeth!"
(A sweeter woman ne'er drew breath
Than my sonne's wife, Elizabeth.)

"The olde sea wall" (he cried) "is downe,
   The rising tide comes on apace,
And boats adrift in yonder towne
   Go sailing uppe the market-place."
He shook as one that looks on death:
"God save you, mother!" straight he saith;
"Where is my wife, Elizabeth?"

"Good sonne, where Lindis winds away
   With her two bairns I marked her long;
And ere yon bells beganne to play
   Afar I heard her milking song."
He looked across the grassy sea,
To right, to left, "Ho Enderby!"
They rang *The Brides of Enderby!*

With that he cried and beat his breast;
   For lo! along the river's bed
A mighty eygre reared his crest,
   And uppe the Lindis raging sped.
It swept with thunderous noises loud;
Shaped like a curling snow-white cloud,
Or like a demon in a shroud.

And rearing Lindis backward pressed
   Shook all her trembling bankes amaine;
Then madly at the eygre's breast
   Flung uppe her weltering walls again.

Then bankes came downe with ruin and rout—
Then beaten foam flew round about—
Then all the mighty floods were out.

So farre, so fast the eygre drave,
　The heart had hardly time to beat,
Before a shallow seething wave
　Sobbed in the grasses at oure feet:
The feet had hardly time to flee
Before it brake against the knee,
And all the world was in the sea.

Upon the roofe we sate that night,
　The noise of bells went sweeping by:
I marked the lofty beacon light
　Stream from the church tower, red and high—
A lurid mark and dread to see;
And awesome bells they were to mee,
That in the dark rang *Enderby*.

They rang the sailor lads to guide
　From roofe to roofe who fearless rowed;
And I—my sonne was at my side,
　And yet the ruddy beacon glowed:
And yet he moaned beneath his breath,
"O come in life, or come in death!
O lost! my love, Elizabeth."

And didst thou visit him no more?
　Thou didst, thou didst my daughter deare;
The waters laid thee at his doore,
　Ere yet the early dawn was clear.
Thy pretty bairns in fast embrace,
The lifted sun shone on thy face,
Downe drifted to thy dwelling-place.

That flow strewed wrecks about the grass,
　That ebbe swept out the flocks to sea;
A fatal ebbe and flow, alas!
　To manye more than myne and mee:

But each will mourn his own (she saith),
And sweeter woman ne'er drew breath
Than my sonne's wife, Elizabeth.

I shall never hear her more
By the reedy Lindis shore,
"Cusha! Cusha! Cusha!" calling,
Ere the early dews be falling;
I shall never hear her song,
"Cusha! Cusha!" all along,
Where the sunny Lindis floweth,
    Goeth, floweth;
From the meads where melick groweth,
When the water winding down,
Onward floweth to the town.

I shall never see her more
Where the reeds and rushes quiver,
    Shiver, quiver;
Stand beside the sobbing river,
Sobbing, throbbing, in its falling,
To the sandy lonesome shore;
I shall never hear her calling,
"Leave your meadow grasses mellow,
    Mellow, mellow;
Quit your cowslips, cowslips yellow;
Come uppe Whitefoot, come uppe Lightfoot;
Quit your pipes of parsley hollow,
    Hollow, hollow;
Come uppe Lightfoot, rise and follow;
    Lightfoot, Whitefoot,
From your clovers lift the head;
Come uppe Jetty, follow, follow,
Jetty, to the milking shed."

ARNOLD, Matthew

MATTHEW ARNOLD (1822–1888), the son of Dr Thomas
Arnold, was born at Laleham, Middlesex, and educated
at Winchester, Rugby and Balliol College, Oxford. He
received a fellowship at Oriel College; but, leaving
Oxford, settled to a Government inspectorship of schools.
The dramatic poems *Empedocles on Etna* and *Tristram and
Iseult, Sohrab and Rustum* and *The Scholar-Gipsy*, his two
best narrative poems, and *Requiescat* were all early com-
positions. From 1857 to 1867 Arnold was Professor of
Poetry at Oxford. *Thyrsis* appeared. Arnold's *Essays in
Criticism, Literature and Dogma, Last Essays on Church
and Religion*—all later work—did much to advance
modernism in religion. He retired from the Civil Service
in 1883 on a Civil List pension and continued writing.
As a master of graceful narrative, Arnold has no superior
among our poets.

From *Empedocles on Etna*

The out-spread world to span
A cord the Gods first slung,
And then the soul of man
There, like a mirror, hung,
And bade the winds through space impel the gusty
    toy.

Hither and thither spins
The wind-borne, mirroring soul:
A thousand glimpses wins,
And never sees a whole;
Looks once, and drives elsewhere, and leaves its last
    employ.

     *   *   *   *

We mortals are no kings
For each of whom to sway
A new-made world up-springs
Meant merely for his play;
No, we are strangers here: the world is from of
    old.

     *   *   *   *

The world's course proves the terms
On which man wins content;
Reason the proof confirms.
We spurn it, and invent
A false course for the world, and for ourselves, false
      powers.

*   *   *   *

We do not what we ought,
What we ought not, we do,
And lean upon the thought
That chance will bring us through;
But our own acts, for good or ill, are mightier
      powers.

Yet, even when man forsakes
All sin,—is just, is pure,
Abandons all which makes
His welfare insecure,—
Other existences there are, that clash with ours.

Like us, the lightning-fires
Love to have scope and play,
The stream, like us, desires
An unimpeded way.
Like us, the Libyan wind delights to roam at large.

Streams will not curb their pride
The just man not to entomb,
Nor lightnings go aside
To leave his virtues room;
Nor is that wind less rough which blows a good
      man's barge.

Nature, with equal mind,
Sees all her sons at play;
Sees man control the wind,
The wind sweep man away;
Allows the proudly-riding and the foundering bark.

And, lastly, though of ours
No weakness spoil our lot,
Though the non-human powers
Of Nature harm us not,
The ill-deeds of other men make often *our* life dark.

What were the wise man's plan?—
Through this sharp, toil-set life,
To fight as best he can,
And win what's won by strife.—
But we an easier way to cheat our pains have found.

Scratched by a fall, with moans
As children of weak age
Lend life to the dumb stones
Whereon to vent their rage,
And bend their little fists, and rate the senseless
    ground;

So, loath to suffer mute,
We, peopling the void air,
Make Gods to whom to impute
The ills we ought to bear;
With God and Fate to rail at, suffering easily.

*   *   *   *

Fools! that so often here
Happiness mock'd our prayer,
I think, might make us fear
A like event elsewhere;
Make us, not fly to dreams, but moderate desire.

*   *   *   *

Is it so small a thing
To have enjoy'd the sun,
To have lived light in the spring,
To have loved, to have thought, to have done;
To have advanced true friends, and beat down
    baffling foes;

That we must feign a bliss
Of doubtful future date,
And while we dream on this,
Lose all our present state,
And relegate to worlds yet distant our repose?

*　　*　　*　　*

I say: Fear not! Life still
Leaves human effort scope.
But, since life teems with ill,
Nurse no extravagant hope;
Because thou must not dream, thou need'st not
　　then despair!

Requiescat

STREW on her roses, roses,
　And never a spray of yew!
In quiet she reposes;
　Ah! would that I did too.

Her mirth the world required;
　She bath'd it in smiles of glee.
But her heart was tired, tired,
　And now they let her be.

Her life was turning, turning,
　In mazes of heat and sound;
But for peace her soul was yearning,
　And now peace laps her round.

Her cabin'd, ample spirit,
　It flutter'd and fail'd for breath.
To-night it doth inherit
　The vasty hall of death.

From *Sohrab and Rustum*

So, on the bloody sand, Sohrab lay dead;
And the great Rustum drew his horseman's cloak
Down o'er his face, and sate by his dead son.
As those black granite pillars, once high-rear'd
By Jemshid in Persepolis, to bear
His house, now 'mid their broken flights of steps
Lie prone, enormous, down the mountain side—
So in the sand lay Rustum by his son.
    And night came down over the solemn waste,
And the two gazing hosts, and that sole pair,
And darken'd all; and a cold fog, with night,
Crept from the Oxus. Soon a hum arose,
As of a great assembly loosed, and fires
Began to twinkle through the fog; for now
Both armies moved to camp, and took their meal;
The Persians took it on the open sands
Southward, only the Tartars by the river marge;
And Rustum and his son were left alone.
    But the majestic River floated on,
Out of the mist and hum of that low land,
Into the frosty starlight, and there moved,
Rejoicing, through the hush'd Chorasmian waste,
Under the solitary moon; he flow'd
Right for the polar star, past Orgunjé,
Brimming, and bright, and large; then sands begin
To hem his watery march, and dam his streams,
And split his currents; that for many a league
The shorn and parcell'd Oxus strains along
Through beds of sand and matted rushy isles—
Oxus, forgetting the bright speed he had
In his high mountain-cradle in Pamere,
A foil'd circuitous wanderer—till at last
The long'd-for dash of waves is heard, and wide
His luminous home of waters opens, bright
And tranquil, from whose floor the new-bathed stars
Emerge, and shine upon the Aral Sea.

The Scholar-Gipsy

"There was very lately a lad in the University of Oxford, who was by his poverty forced to leave his studies there; and at last to join himself to a company of vagabond gipsies. Among these extravagant people, by the insinuating subtilty of his carriage, he quickly got so much of their love and esteem as that they discovered to him their mystery. After he had been a pretty while exercised in the trade, there chanced to ride by a couple of scholars, who had formerly been of his acquaintance. They quickly spied out their old friend among the gipsies; and he gave them an account of the necessity which drove him to that kind of life, and told them that the people he went with were not such impostors as they were taken for, but that they had a traditional kind of learning among them, and could do wonders by the power of imagination, their fancy binding that of others: that himself had learned much of their art, and when he had compassed the whole secret, he intended, he said, to leave their company, and give the world an account of what he had learned."

GLANVIL'S *Vanity of Dogmatizing*, 1661.

Go, for they call you, shepherd, from the hill;
  Go, shepherd, and untie the wattled cotes!
    No longer leave thy wistful flock unfed,
  Nor let thy bawling fellows rack their throats,
    Nor the cropp'd herbage shoot another head.
      But when the fields are still,
  And the tired men and dogs all gone to rest,
    And only the white sheep are sometimes seen
    Cross and recross the strips of moon-blanch'd
        green;
  Come, shepherd, and again begin the quest!

Here, where the reaper was at work of late—
  In this high field's dark corner, where he leaves
    His coat, his basket, and his earthen cruise,
  And in the sun all morning binds the sheaves,
    Then here, at noon, comes back his stores to
      use—
      Here will I sit and wait,
  While to my ear from uplands far away
    The bleating of the folded flocks is borne,
    With distant cries of reapers in the corn—
All the live murmur of a summer's day.

Screen'd is this nook o'er the high, half-reap'd
field,
And here till sun-down, shepherd! will I be.
Through the thick corn the scarlet poppies
peep,
And round green roots and yellowing stalks I see
Pale pink convolvulus in tendrils creep;
And air-swept lindens yield
Their scent, and rustle down their perfumed
showers
Of bloom on the bent grass where I am laid,
And bower me from the August sun with
shade;
And the eye travels down to Oxford's towers.

And near me on the grass lies Glanvil's book—
Come, let me read the oft-read tale again!
The story of the Oxford scholar poor,
Of pregnant parts and quick inventive brain,
Who, tired of knocking at preferment's door,
One summer-morn forsook
His friends, and went to learn the gipsy lore,
And roam'd the world with that wild brother-
hood,
And came, as most men deem'd, to little good,
But came to Oxford and his friends no more.

But once, years after, in the country-lanes,
Two scholars, whom at college erst he knew,
Met him, and of his way of life enquired;
Whereat he answer'd, that the gipsy-crew,
His mates, had arts to rule as they desired
The workings of men's brains,
And they can bind them to what thoughts they
will.
"And I," he said, "the secret of their art,
When fully learn'd, will to the world impart;
But it needs heaven-sent moments for this skill."

This said, he left them, and return'd no more.—
　But rumours hung about the country-side,
　　That the lost Scholar long was seen to stray,
　Seen by rare glimpses, pensive and tongue-tied,
　　In hat of antique shape, and cloak of grey,
　　　The same the gipsies wore.
　Shepherds had met him on the Hurst in spring;
　　At some lone alehouse in the Berkshire moors,
　　On the warm ingle-bench, the smock-frock'd
　　　boors
　Had found him seated at their entering,

But, 'mid their drink and clatter, he would fly.
　And I myself seem half to know thy looks,
　　And put the shepherds, wanderer! on thy
　　　trace;
　And boys who in lone wheatfields scare the
　　　rooks
　　I ask if thou hast pass'd their quiet place;
　　　Or in my boat I lie
　Moor'd to the cool bank in the summer-heats,
　　'Mid wide grass meadows which the sunshine
　　　fills,
　　And watch the warm, green-muffled Cumner
　　　hills,
　And wonder if thou haunt'st their shy retreats.

For most, I know, thou lov'st retired ground!
　Thee at the ferry Oxford riders blithe,
　　Returning home on summer-nights, have met
　Crossing the stripling Thames at Bab-lock-hithe,
　　Trailing in the cool stream thy fingers wet,
　　　As the punt's rope chops round;
　And leaning backward in a pensive dream,
　　And fostering in thy lap a heap of flowers
　　Pluck'd in shy fields and distant Wychwood
　　　bowers,
　And thine eyes resting on the moonlit stream.

And then they land, and thou art seen no more!—
  Maidens who from the distant hamlets come
    To dance around the Fyfield elm in May,
  Oft through the darkening fields have seen thee
      roam,
    Or cross a stile into the public way.
      Oft thou hast given them store
  Of flowers—the frail-leaf'd, white anemony,
    Dark bluebells drench'd with dews of summer
      eves,
    And purple orchises with spotted leaves—
  But none hath words she can report of thee.

And, above Godstow Bridge, when hay-time's here
  In June, and many a scythe in sunshine flames,
    Men who through those wide fields of breezy
      grass
  Where black-wing'd swallows haunt the glittering
      Thames,
    To bathe in the abandon'd lasher pass,
      Have often pass'd thee near
  Sitting upon the river bank o'ergrown;
    Mark'd thine outlandish garb, thy figure spare,
    Thy dark vague eyes, and soft abstracted air—
  But, when they came from bathing, thou wast
      gone!

At some lone homestead in the Cumner hills,
  Where at her open door the housewife darns,
    Thou hast been seen, or hanging on a gate
  To watch the threshers in the mossy barns.
    Children, who early range these slopes and late
      For cresses from the rills,
  Have known thee eyeing, all an April-day,
    The springing pastures and the feeding kine;
    And mark'd thee, when the stars come out and
      shine,
  Through the long dewy grass move slow away.

In autumn, on the skirts of Bagley Wood—
　Where most the gipsies by the turf-edg'd way
　　Pitch their smok'd tents, and every bush you
　　　see
　With scarlet patches tagg'd and shreds of grey,
　　Above the forest-ground call'd Thessaly—
　　　The blackbird, picking food,
　Sees thee, nor stops his meal, nor fears at all;
　　So often has he known thee past him stray,
　　Rapt, twirling in thy hand a wither'd spray,
And waiting for the spark from heaven to fall.

And once, in winter, on the causeway chill
　Where home through flooded fields foot-travellers
　　　go,
　　Have I not pass'd thee on the wooden bridge
　Wrapt in thy cloak and battling with the snow,
　　Thy face tow'rd Hinksey and its wintry ridge?
　　　And thou hast climb'd the hill
　And gain'd the white brow of the Cumner range;
　　Turn'd once to watch, while thick the snow-
　　　flakes fall,
　　The line of festal light in Christ-Church hall—
Then sought thy straw in some sequester'd
　　　grange.

But what—I dream! Two hundred years are flown
　Since first thy story ran through Oxford halls,
　　And the grave Glanvil did the tale inscribe
　That thou wert wander'd from the studious walls
　　To learn strange arts, and join a gipsy-tribe;
　　　And thou from earth art gone
　Long since, and in some quiet churchyard laid—
　　Some country nook, where o'er thy unknown
　　　grave
　　Tall grasses and white flowering nettles wave,
Under a dark red-fruited yew-tree's shade.

*　　*　　*　　*

O born in days when wits were fresh and clear,
  And life ran gaily as the sparkling Thames;
    Before this strange disease of modern life,
  With its sick hurry, its divided aims,
    Its heads o'ertax'd, its palsied hearts, was rife—
      Fly hence, our contact fear!
  Still fly, plunge deeper in the bowering wood!
    Averse, as Dido did with gesture stern
    From her false friend's approach in Hades
      turn,
  Wave us away, and keep thy solitude!

Still nursing the unconquerable hope,
  Still clutching the inviolable shade,
    With a free onward impulse brushing through,
  By night, the silver'd branches of the glade—
    Far on the forest-skirts, where none pursue,
      On some mild pastoral slope
  Emerge, and resting on the moonlit pales
    Freshen thy flowers as in former years,
    With dew, or listen with enchanted ears,
  From the dark dingles, to the nightingales!

But fly our paths, our feverish contact fly!
  For strong the infection of our mental strife,
    Which, though it gives no bliss, yet spoils for
      rest;
  And we should win thee from thy own fair life,
    Like us distracted, and like us unblest.
      Soon, soon thy cheer would die,
  Thy hopes grow timorous, and unfix'd thy
      powers,
    And thy clear aims be cross and shifting
      made;
    And then thy glad perennial youth would
      fade,
  Fade, and grow old at last, and die like ours.

Then fly our greetings, fly our speech and smiles!
  —As some grave Tyrian trader, from the sea,
    Descried at sunrise an emerging prow
  Lifting the cool-hair'd creepers stealthily,
    The fringes of a southward-facing brow
      Among the Aegean isles;
  And saw the merry Grecian coaster come,
    Freighted with amber grapes, and Chian wine,
    Green bursting figs, and tunnies steep'd in
      brine—
  And knew the intruders on his ancient home,

The young light-hearted masters of the waves—
  And snatch'd his rudder, and shook out more sail;
    And day and night held on indignantly
  O'er the blue Midland waters with the gale,
    Betwixt the Syrtes and soft Sicily,
      To where the Atlantic raves
  Outside the western straits; and unbent sails
    There, where down cloudy cliffs, through
      sheets of foam,
    Shy traffickers, the dark Iberians come;
  And on the beach undid his corded bales.

CORY, William Johnson

WILLIAM JOHNSON CORY (1823–1892) was born at Tor-
rington, Devon, and educated at Eton and King's College,
Cambridge. For a time he was a master at Eton. He
inherited an estate, assumed the name Cory and retired.

Mimnermus in Church

YOU promise heavens free from strife,
  Pure truth, and perfect change of will;
But sweet, sweet is this human life,
  So sweet, I fain would breathe it still;
Your chilly stars I can forgo,
This warm kind world is all I know.

You say there is no substance here,
  One great reality above:
Back from that void I shrink in fear,
  And child-like hide myself in love:
Show me what angels feel. Till then,
I cling, a mere weak man, to men.

You bid me lift my mean desires
  From faltering lips and fitful veins
To sexless souls, ideal quires,
  Unwearied voices, wordless strains:
My mind with fonder welcome owns
One dear dead friend's remembered tones.

Forsooth the present we must give
  To that which cannot pass away;
All beauteous things for which we live
  By laws of time and space decay.
But oh, the very reason why
I clasp them, is because they die.

PATMORE, Coventry Kersey Dighton

COVENTRY KERSEY DIGHTON PATMORE (1823–1896) was
born at Woodford, Essex, and educated privately. He
received appointment in the printed book department of
the British Museum. He is best known for his highly
unequal poem *The Angel in the House* and for his sympathy with the Pre-Raphaelite Movement. He turned to
Roman Catholicism and made a very bad convert.

Magna est Veritas

HERE, in this little Bay,
Full of tumultuous life and great repose,
Where, twice a day,
The purposeless, glad ocean comes and goes,
Under high cliffs, and far from the huge town,
I sit me down.

For want of me the world's course will not fail:
When all its work is done, the lie shall rot;
The truth is great, and shall prevail,
When none cares whether it prevail or not.

ROSSETTI, Dante Gabriel

DANTE GABRIEL ROSSETTI (1828–1882) was born in
London, of Italian parentage, received part of his
education at King's College, London, and turned to art.
By 1848, *The Blessed Damozel* was written. Rossetti
studied painting under Ford Madox Brown and was the
founder of the "Pre-Raphaelite" school. The claim of that
school to serious attention was advanced by Ruskin, hotly
disputed by others; and Pre-Raphaelitism still continues
to please and to annoy. Rossetti became a victim of
chloral; but, toward the end of his life, when most
completely enslaved to the drug, he could produce such
striking verse as *The White Ship*.

From *The Choice*

Think thou and act; tomorrow thou shalt die.
    Outstretched in the sun's warmth upon the shore,
    Thou say'st "Man's measured path is all gone o'er:
Up all his years, steeply, with strain and sigh,
Man clomb until he touched the truth; and I,
    Even I, am he whom it was destined for."
    How should this be? Art thou then so much
        more
Than they who sowed, that thou shouldst reap
        thereby?

Nay, come up hither. From this wave-washed
        mound
    Unto the furthest flood-brim look with me;
Then reach on with thy thought till it be drown'd
    Miles and miles distant though the grey line be,
And though thy soul sail leagues and leagues
        beyond,—
    Still, leagues beyond those leagues, there is more
        sea.

ROSSETTI, Christina Georgina

CHRISTINA GEORGINA ROSSETTI (1830–1894), born in London, of Italian parentage, was educated at home. Kept from Roman Catholicism by a strong Italian patriotism, she sought refuge in High Church Anglicanism, refused a suitor whom she loved and developed a melancholy which colours her poetry. *Goblin Market, and other Poems*, published in 1862, was early work and her best. Christina Rossetti's lyrics are often of exquisite beauty; and she has right to a high place among English poets.

Song

WHEN I am dead, my dearest,
  Sing no sad songs for me;
Plant thou no roses at my head,
  Nor shady cypress tree:
Be the green grass above me
  With showers and dewdrops wet:
And if thou wilt, remember,
  And if thou wilt, forget.

I shall not see the shadows,
  I shall not feel the rain;
I shall not hear the nightingale
  Sing on as if in pain:
And dreaming through the twilight
  That doth not rise nor set,
Haply I may remember,
  And haply may forget.

A Birthday

MY heart is like a singing bird
  Whose nest is in a watered shoot;
My heart is like an apple-tree
  Whose boughs are bent with thickset fruit;

My heart is like a rainbow shell
  That paddles in a halcyon sea;
My heart is gladder than all these
  Because my love is come to me.

Raise me a dais of silk and down;
  Hang it with vair and purple dyes;
Carve it in doves, and pomegranates,
  And peacocks with a hundred eyes;
Work it in gold and silver grapes,
  In leaves and silver fleurs-de-lys;
Because the birthday of my life
  Is come, my love is come to me.

Up-hill

DOES the road wind up-hill all the way?
  Yes, to the very end.
Will the day's journey take the whole long day?
  From morn to night, my friend.

But is there for the night a resting-place?
  A roof for when the slow dark hours begin.
May not the darkness hide it from my face?
  You cannot miss that inn.

Shall I meet other wayfarers at night?
  Those who have gone before.
Then must I knock, or call when just in sight?
  They will not keep you standing at that door.

Shall I find comfort, travel-sore and weak?
  Of labour you shall find the sum.
Will there be beds for me and all who seek?
  Yea, beds for all who come.

DIXON, Richard Watson

RICHARD WATSON DIXON (1833–1900), born at Islington, was educated at King Edward's School, Birmingham, and Pembroke College, Oxford. Dixon took orders, became minor canon and honorary librarian of Carlisle. His principal work was a *History of the Church of England from the Abolition of the Roman Jurisdiction*. His *Selected Poems* were edited in 1909 by Bridges.

Song

THE feathers of the willow
Are half of them grown yellow
   Above the swelling stream;
And ragged are the bushes,
And rusty now the rushes,
   And wild the clouded gleam.

The thistle now is older,
His stalk begins to moulder,
   His head is white as snow;
The branches all are barer,
The linnet's song is rarer,
   The robin pipeth now.

THOMSON, James

JAMES THOMSON (1834–1882), born at Port-Glasgow, Renfrewshire, was early orphaned. He was educated at the Royal Caledonian Asylum and at the Military Asylum, Chelsea. Whilst assistant Army Schoolmaster at Ballincollig, near Cork, he fell passionately in love with a girl whose early death started the poet's despondency. In Ballincollig he also met Charles Bradlaugh, who, on Thomson's discharge from the Army in 1862, found work for him. *The City of Dreadful Night*, reprinted from Bradlaugh's *The National Reformer* in 1880, won Thomson recognition. A victim of drink, Thomson died homeless. The power of Thomson's thought and the grandeur of his imagery are beyond question; the uneven character of his poetry is a grave defect.

From *The City of Dreadful Night*

"THE world rolls round for ever like a mill;
It grinds out death and life and good and ill;
It has no purpose, heart or mind or will.

"While air of Space and Time's full river flow
The mill must blindly whirl unresting so:
It may be wearing out, but who can know?

"Man might know one thing were his sight less dim;
That it whirls not to suit his petty whim,
That it is quite indifferent to him.

"Nay, does it treat him harshly as he saith?
It grinds him some slow years of bitter breath,
Then grinds him back into eternal death."

*   *   *   *

How the moon triumphs through the endless nights!
  How the stars throb and glitter as they wheel
Their thick processions of supernal lights
  Around the blue vault obdurate as steel!
And men regard with passionate awe and yearning
The mighty marching and the golden burning,
  And think the heavens respond to what they feel.

*   *   *   *

With such a living light these dead eyes shine,
  These eyes of sightless heaven, that as we gaze
We read a pity, tremulous, divine,
  Or cold majestic scorn in their pure rays:
Fond man! they are not haughty, are not tender;
There is no heart or mind in all their splendour,
  They thread mere puppets all their marvellous
    maze.

If we could near them with the flight unflown,
  We should but find them worlds as sad as this,
Or suns all self-consuming like our own
  Enringed by planet worlds as much amiss:
They wax and wane through fusion and confusion;
The spheres eternal are a grand illusion,
  The empyréan is a void abyss.

MORRIS, William

WILLIAM MORRIS (1834–1896), born at Walthamstow, was educated privately, at Marlborough College and at Exeter College, Oxford, where he met Burne-Jones. Later, he made the acquaintance of Rossetti, on whose advice he became an artist. In 1858, *The Defence of Guenevere* appeared, practically unnoticed. Morris abandoned painting for decoration and founded a firm. *The Life and Death of Jason*, 1867, won fame. *The Earthly Paradise* and Icelandic translations were written, followed by *Sigurd the Volsung*. For some years, Morris gave himself up to Socialist propaganda. The prose work, *A Dream of John Ball*, was produced. During Morris's last years, he brought out a series of prose romances exquisitely printed at his private press. *News from Nowhere* came out in 1890. There is little doubt that, had he so desired, Morris might have become Poet Laureate, on Tennyson's death. Morris naturally challenges comparison with Arnold from whom he is different but to whom he is not inferior.

The Haystack in the Floods

HAD she come all the way for this,
To part at last without a kiss?
Yea, had she borne the dirt and rain
That her own eyes might see him slain
Beside the haystack in the floods?

Along the dripping leafless woods,
The stirrup touching either shoe,
She rode astride as troopers do;
With kirtle kilted to her knee,
To which the mud splash'd wretchedly;
And the wet dripp'd from every tree
Upon her head and heavy hair,
And on her eyelids broad and fair;
The tears and rain ran down her face.
By fits and starts they rode apace,
And very often was his place
Far off from her; he had to ride
Ahead, to see what might betide

When the roads cross'd; and sometimes, when
There rose a murmuring from his men,
Had to turn back with promises;
Ah me! she had but little ease;
And often for pure doubt and dread
She sobb'd, made giddy in the head
By the swift riding; while, for cold,
Her slender fingers scarce could hold
The wet reins; yea, and scarcely, too,
She felt the foot within her shoe
Against the stirrup: all for this,
To part at last without a kiss
Beside the haystack in the floods.

For when they near'd that old soak'd hay,
They saw across the only way
That Judas, Godmar, and the three
Red running lions dismally
Grinn'd from his pennon, under which,
In one straight line along the ditch,
They counted thirty heads.

               So then,
While Robert turn'd round to his men,
She saw at once the wretched end,
And, stooping down, tried hard to rend
Her coif the wrong way from her head,
And hid her eyes; while Robert said:
"Nay, love, 'tis scarcely two to one,
At Poictiers where we made them run
So fast—why, sweet my love, good cheer,
The Gascon frontier is so near,
Nought after this."

              But, "O," she said,
"My God! my God! I have to tread
The long way back without you; then
The court at Paris; those six men;

The gratings of the Chatelet;
The swift Seine on some rainy day
Like this, and people standing by,
And laughing, while my weak hands try
To recollect how strong men swim.
All this, or else a life with him,
For which I should be damned at last,
Would God that this next hour were past!"

He answer'd not, but cried his cry,
"St George for Marny!" cheerily;
And laid his hand upon her rein.
Alas! no man of all his train
Gave back that cheery cry again;
And, while for rage his thumb beat fast
Upon his sword-hilt, some one cast
About his neck a kerchief long
And bound him.

   Then they went along
To Godmar; who said: "Now, Jehane,
Your lover's life is on the wane
So fast, that, if this very hour
You yield not as my paramour,
He will not see the rain leave off—
Nay, keep your tongue from gibe and scoff,
Sir Robert, or I slay you now."

She laid her hand upon her brow,
Then gazed upon the palm, as though
She thought her forehead bled, and—"No."
She said, and turned her head away,
As there were nothing else to say,
And everything were settled: red
Grew Godmar's face from chin to head:
"Jehane, on yonder hill there stands
My castle, guarding well my lands:
What hinders me from taking you,
And doing what I list to do

To your fair wilful body, while
Your knight lies dead?"

                    A wicked smile
Wrinkled her face, her lips grew thin,
A long way out she thrust her chin:
"You know that I should strangle you
While you were sleeping; or bite through
Your throat, by God's help—ah!" she said,
"Lord Jesus, pity your poor maid!
For in such wise they hem me in,
I cannot choose but sin and sin,
Whatever happens: yet I think
They could not make me eat or drink,
And so should I just reach my rest."
"Nay, if you do not my behest,
O Jehane! though I love you well,"
Said Godmar, "would I fail to tell
All that I know?" "Foul lies," she said.
"Eh? lies, my Jehane? by God's head,
At Paris folks would deem them true!
Do you know, Jehane, they cry for you,
'Jehane the brown! Jehane the brown!
Give us Jehane to burn or drown!'—
Eh—gag me, Robert!—sweet my friend,
This were indeed a piteous end
For those long fingers, and long feet,
And long neck, and smooth shoulders sweet;
An end that few men would forget
That saw it—So, an hour yet:
Consider, Jehane, which to take
Of life or death!"

                So, scarce awake,
Dismounting, did she leave that place,
And totter some yards: with her face
Turn'd upward to the sky she lay,
Her head on a wet heap of hay,

And fell asleep: and while she slept,
And did not dream, the minutes crept
Round to the twelve again; but she,
Being waked at last, sigh'd quietly,
And strangely childlike came, and said:
"I will not." Straightway Godmar's head,
As though it hung on strong wires, turn'd
Most sharply round, and his face burn'd.

For Robert—both his eyes were dry,
He could not weep, but gloomily
He seem'd to watch the rain; yea, too,
His lips were firm; he tried once more
To touch her lips; she reached out, sore
And vain desire so tortured them,
The poor grey lips, and now the hem
Of his sleeve brush'd them.

                    With a start
Up Godmar rose, thrust them apart;
From Robert's throat he loosed the bands
Of silk and mail; with empty hands
Held out, she stood and gazed, and saw,
The long bright blade without a flaw
Glide out from Godmar's sheath, his hand
In Robert's hair; she saw him bend
Back Robert's head; she saw him send
The thin steel down; the blow told well,
Right backward the knight Robert fell,
And moan'd as dogs do, being half dead,
Unwitting, as I deem: so then
Godmar turn'd grinning to his men,
Who ran, some five or six, and beat
His head to pieces at their feet.

Then Godmar turn'd again and said:
"So, Jehane, the first fitte is read!
Take note, my lady, that your way
Lies backward to the Chatelet!"

She shook her head and gazed awhile
At her cold hands with a rueful smile,
As though this thing had made her mad.

This was the parting that they had
Beside the haystack in the floods.

SWINBURNE, Algernon Charles

ALGERNON CHARLES SWINBURNE (1837–1909), born in
London of Northumbrian descent, was educated by a
tutor and at Eton and Balliol College, Oxford. At college,
he became an atheist and a republican. He left Balliol
without taking a degree. *Atalanta in Calydon* found
instant success in 1865. *Poems and Ballads*, *Songs before
Sunrise* and further *Poems and Ballads* added to Swinburne's reputation. With health broken by excesses, he
retired to Putney, tended by Theodore Watts-Dunton.
There he died. Swinburne wrote a measured music. His
defects proceed from a lack of character.

From *Atalanta in Calydon*

WHEN the hounds of spring are on winter's traces,
    The mother of months in meadow or plain
Fills the shadows and windy places
    With lisp of leaves and ripple of rain;
And the brown bright nightingale amorous
Is half assuaged for Itylus,
For the Thracian ships and the foreign faces,
    The tongueless vigil, and all the pain.

Come with bows bent and with emptying of quivers,
    Maiden most perfect, lady of light,
With a noise of winds and many rivers,
    With a clamour of waters, and with might;
Bind on thy sandals, O thou most fleet,
Over the splendour and speed of thy feet;
For the faint east quickens, the wan west shivers,
    Round the feet of the day and the feet of the night.

Where shall we find her, how shall we sing to her,
    Fold our hands round her knees, and cling?
O that man's heart were as fire and could spring to
        her,
    Fire, or the strength of the streams that spring!
For the stars and the winds are unto her
As raiment, as songs of the harp-player;
For the risen stars and the fallen cling to her,
    And the southwest-wind and the west wind
        sing.

For winter's rains and ruins are over,
    And all the season of snows and sins;
The days dividing lover and lover,
    The light that loses, the night that wins;
And time remembered is grief forgotten,
And frosts are slain and flowers begotten,
And in green underwood and cover
    Blossom by blossom the spring begins.

The full streams feed on flower of rushes,
    Ripe grasses trammel a travelling foot,
The faint fresh flame of the young year flushes
    From leaf to flower and flower to fruit;
And fruit and leaf are as gold and fire,
And the oat is heard above the lyre,
And the hoofèd heel of a satyr crushes
    The chestnut-husk at the chestnut-root.

And Pan by noon and Bacchus by night,
    Fleeter of foot than the fleet-foot kid,
Follows with dancing and fills with delight
    The Mænad and the Bassarid;
And soft as lips that laugh and hide
The laughing leaves of the trees divide,
And screen from seeing and leave in sight
    The god pursuing, the maiden hid.

The ivy falls with the Bacchanal's hair
 Over her eyebrows hiding her eyes;
The wild vine slipping down leaves bare
 Her bright breast shortening into sighs;
The wild vine slips with the weight of its leaves,
But the berried ivy catches and cleaves
To the limbs that glitter, the feet that scare
 The wolf that follows, the fawn that flies.

The Garden of Proserpine

HERE, where the world is quiet;
 Here, where all trouble seems
Dead winds' and spent waves' riot
 In doubtful dreams of dreams;
I watch the green field growing
For reaping folk and sowing,
For harvest-time and mowing,
 A sleepy world of streams.

I am tired of tears and laughter,
 And men that laugh and weep;
Of what may come hereafter
 For men that sow to reap:
I am weary of days and hours,
Blown buds of barren flowers,
Desires and dreams and powers
 And everything but sleep.

Here life has death for neighbour,
 And far from eye or ear
Wan waves and wet winds labour,
 Weak ships and spirits steer;
They drive adrift, and whither
They wot not who make thither;
But no such winds blow hither,
 And no such things grow here.

No growth of moor or coppice,
　No heather-flower or vine,
But bloomless buds of poppies,
　Green grapes of Proserpine,
Pale beds of blowing rushes,
Where no leaf blooms or blushes
Save this whereout she crushes
　For dead men deadly wine.

Pale, without name or number,
　In fruitless fields of corn,
They bow themselves and slumber
　All night till light is born;
And like a soul belated,
In hell and heaven unmated,
By cloud and mist abated
　Comes out of darkness morn.

Though one were strong as seven,
　He too with death shall dwell,
Nor wake with wings in heaven,
　Nor weep for pains in hell;
Though one were fair as roses,
His beauty clouds and closes;
And well though love reposes,
　In the end it is not well.

Pale, beyond porch and portal,
　Crowned with calm leaves, she stands
Who gathers all things mortal
　With cold immortal hands;
Her languid lips are sweeter
Than love's who fears to greet her
To men that mix and meet her
　From many times and lands.

She waits for each and other,
　She waits for all men born;
Forgets the earth her mother,
　The life of fruits and corn;

And spring and seed and swallow
Take wing for her and follow
Where summer song rings hollow
    And flowers are put to scorn.

There go the loves that wither,
    The old loves with wearier wings;
And all dead years draw thither,
    And all disastrous things;
Dead dreams of days forsaken,
Blind buds that snows have shaken,
Wild leaves that winds have taken,
    Red strays of ruined springs.

We are not sure of sorrow,
    And joy was never sure;
To-day will die to-morrow;
    Time stoops to no man's lure;
And love, grown faint and fretful,
With lips but half regretful
Sighs, and with eyes forgetful
    Weeps that no loves endure.

From too much love of living,
    From hope and fear set free,
We thank with brief thanksgiving
    Whatever gods may be
That no life lives for ever;
That dead men rise up never;
That even the weariest river
    Winds somewhere safe to sea.

Then star nor sun shall waken,
    Nor any change of light:
Nor sound of waters shaken,
    Nor any sound or sight:
Nor wintry leaves nor vernal,
Nor days nor things diurnal;
Only the sleep eternal
    In an eternal night.

DOBSON, Henry Austin

HENRY AUSTIN DOBSON (1840–1921), born at Plymouth, was educated at Beaumaris Grammar School, at a Coventry private school and at Strasbourg (then French). He was attached to the Board of Trade. *Vignettes in Rhyme* appeared in 1873. Other volumes followed. Dobson is noted for his eighteenth-century biographies.

A Ballad to Queen Elizabeth of the Spanish Armada

KING PHILIP had vaunted his claims;
    He had sworn for a year he would sack us;
With an army of heathenish names
    He was coming to fagot and stack us;
    Like the thieves of the sea he would track us,
And shatter our ships on the main;
    But we had bold Neptune to back us,—
And where are the galleons of Spain?

His caracks were christened of dames
    To the kirtles whereof he would tack us;
With his saints and his gilded stern-frames,
    He had thought like an egg-shell to crack us:
    Now Howard may get to his Flaccus,
And Drake to his Devon again,
    And Hawkins bowl rubbers to Bacchus,—
For where are the galleons of Spain?

Let his Majesty hang to St James
    The axe that he whetted to hack us;
He must play at some lustier games
    Or at sea he can hope to out-thwack us;
    To his mines of Peru he would pack us
To tug at his bullet and chain;
    Alas! that his Greatness should lack us!—
But where are the galleons of Spain?

Envoy

Gloriana!—the Don may attack us
Whenever his stomach be fain;
    He must reach us before he can rack us,
And where are the galleons of Spain?

HARDY, Thomas

THOMAS HARDY (O.M.) (1840–1928) was born at Bock-hampton, Stinsford, Dorset, and educated in Dorchester and at King's College, London. He successfully studied architecture but desired a literary career. Poetry attracted him but promised no pay. So Hardy first wrote novels. Of those *The Return of the Native, Tess of the d'Urbervilles* and *Jude the Obscure* are usually adjudged the finest. Fierce criticism of the "immorality" of *Jude* followed. Hardy turned to the production of *The Dynasts* (published by 1908), with the exception of Shelley's *Prometheus Unbound*, the only epic drama in the language. All the while Hardy had penned poetry; but the years from 1908 were especially devoted to the publication of verse. The remains of Hardy, though he had expressed a wish for country burial, were, to the surprise of many, placed in Westminster Abbey. Nobody disputes the station of Hardy among the prophets. It is likely that, as a novelist, Hardy will be regarded as our greatest; that, among dramatists, he will be accorded rank as the true successor, but not the copyist, of Shakespeare, the co-equal of the author of the *Cenci*; that the unimitative and frequently harsh music of his verse will give him lasting place among English poets.

Friends Beyond

WILLIAM DEWY, Tranter[1] Reuben, Farmer Ledlow
    late at plough,
      Robert's kin, and John's, and Ned's,
And the Squire, and Lady Susan, lie in Mellstock
    churchyard now!

"Gone," I call them, gone for good, that group of
    local hearts and heads;
      Yet at mothy curfew-tide,
And at midnight when the noon-heat breathes it
    back from walls and leads,

They've a way of whispering to me—fellow-wight
    who yet abide—
      In the muted, measured note
Of a ripple under archways, or a lone cave's stilli-
    cide[2]:

    [1] Carrier.   [2] fall of drops.

"We have triumphed: this achievement turns the
    bane to antidote,
      Unsuccesses to success,
Many thought-worn eves and morrows to a morrow
    free of thought.

No more need we corn and clothing, feel of old
    terrestrial stress;
      Chill detraction stirs no sigh;
Fear of death has even bygone us: death gave all
    that we possess."

W. D.—"Ye mid burn the old bass-viol that I set
    such value by."
    Squire.—"You may hold the manse in fee,
You may wed my spouse, may let my children's
    memory of me die."

Lady S.—"You may have my rich brocades, my
    laces; take each household key;
      Ransack coffer, desk, bureau;
Quiz the few poor treasures hid there, con the
    letters kept by me."

Far.—"Ye mid zell my favourite heifer, ye mid let
    the charlock grow,
      Foul the grinterns,[1] give up thrift."
Far. Wife.—"If ye break my best blue china,
    children, I shan't care or ho."[2]

All.—"We've no wish to hear the tidings, how the
    people's fortunes shift;
      What your daily doings are;
Who are wedded, born, divided; if your lives beat
    slow or swift.

"Curious not the least are we if our intents you
    make or mar,
      If you quire to our old tune,
If the City stage still passes, if the weirs still roar
    afar."

[1] compartments of a granary.   [2] heed.

—Thus, with very gods' composure, freed those
      crosses late and soon
    Which, in life, the Trine allow
(Why, none witteth), and ignoring all that haps
      beneath the moon,

William Dewy, Tranter Reuben, Farmer Ledlow
      late at plough,
    Robert's kin, and John's, and Ned's,
And the Squire, and Lady Susan, murmur mildly
      to me now.

Lausanne

In Gibbon's old Garden: 11–12 p.m. June 27, 1897

(The 110th anniversary of the completion of the "Decline
and Fall" at the same hour and place.)

    A SPIRIT seems to pass,
  Formal in pose, but grave withal and grand:
  He contemplates a volume in his hand,
And far lamps fleck him through the thin acacias.

    Anon the book is closed,
  With "It is finished!" And at the alley's end
  He turns, and when on me his glances bend
As from the Past comes speech—small, muted, yet
      composed.

    "How fares the Truth now?—Ill?
  —Do pens but slily further her advance?
  May one not speed her but in phrase askance?
Do scribes aver the Comic to be Reverend still?

    "Still rule those minds on earth
  At whom sage Milton's wormwood words were
      hurled
 'Truth like a bastard comes into the world
Never without ill-fame to him who gives her birth'?"

In Time of " The Breaking of Nations "[1]

I

ONLY a man harrowing clods
  In a slow silent walk
With an old horse that stumbles and nods
  Half asleep as they stalk.

II

Only thin smoke without flame
  From the heaps of couch-grass;
Yet this will go onward the same
  Though Dynasties pass.

III

Yonder a maid and her wight
  Come whispering by:
War's annals will cloud into night
  Ere their story die.

Afterwards

WHEN the Present has latched its postern behind
    my tremulous stay,
  And the May month flaps its glad green leaves
    like wings,
Delicate-filmed as new-spun silk, will the neigh-
    bours say,
  "He was a man who used to notice such things"?

If it be in the dusk when, like an eyelid's soundless
    blink,
  The dewfall-hawk comes crossing the shades to
    alight
Upon the wind-warped upland thorn, a gazer may
    think,
  "To him this must have been a familiar sight."

[1] Jer. li, 20.

If I pass during some nocturnal blackness, mothy
      and warm,
  When the hedgehog travels furtively over the
      lawn,
One may say, "He strove that such innocent
      creatures should come to no harm,
  But he could do little for them; and now he is
      gone."

If, when hearing that I have been stilled at last,
      they stand at the door,
  Watching the full-starred heavens that winter
      sees,
Will this thought rise on those who will meet my
      face no more,
  "He was one who had an eye for such
      mysteries"?

And will any say when my bell of quittance is
      heard in the gloom,
  And a crossing breeze cuts a pause in its out-
      rollings,
Till they rise again, as they were a new bell's boom,
  "He hears it not now, but used to notice such
      things"?

Weathers

I

THIS is the weather the cuckoo likes,
      And so do I;
When showers betumble the chestnut spikes,
      And nestlings fly:
And the little brown nightingale bills his best,
And they sit outside at "The Travellers' Rest,"
And maids come forth sprig-muslin drest,
And citizens dream of the south and west,
      And so do I.

This is the weather the shepherd shuns,
    And so do I;
When beeches drip in browns and duns,
    And thresh, and ply;
And hill-hid tides throb, throe on throe,
And meadow rivulets overflow,
And drops on gate-bars hang in a row,
And rooks in families homeward go,
    And so do I.

From the *After Scene* of *The Dynasts*

Semichorus I of the Pities (*aerial music*)

To Thee whose eye all Nature owns,
Who hurlest Dynasts from their thrones,[1]
And liftest those of low estate
We sing, with Her men consecrate!

Semichorus II

Yea, Great and Good, Thee, Thee, we hail,
Who shak'st the strong, Who shield'st the frail,
Who hadst not shaped such souls as we
If tender mercy lacked in Thee!

Semichorus I

Though times be when the mortal moan
Seems unascending to Thy throne,
Though seers do not as yet explain
Why Suffering sobs to Thee in vain;

Semichorus II

We hold that Thy unscanted scope
Affords a food for final Hope,
That mild-eyed Prescience ponders nigh
Life's loom, to lull it by-and-by.

---

[1] καθεῖλε ΔΥΝΆΣΤΑΣ ἀπὸ θρόνων—*Magnificat.*

Semichorus I

Therefore we quire to highest height
The Wellwiller, the kindly Might
That balances the Vast for weal,
That purges us by wounds to heal.

Semichorus II

The systemed suns the skies enscroll
Obey Thee in their rhythmic roll,
Ride radiantly at Thy command,
Are darkened by Thy masterhand!

Semichorus I

And these pale panting multitudes
Seen surging here, their moils, their moods,
All shall "fulfil their joy" in Thee,
In Thee abide eternally!

Semichorus II

Exultant adoration give
The Alone, through Whom all living live,
The Alone, in Whom all dying die,
Whose means the End shall justify! Amen.[1]

O'SHAUGHNESSY, Arthur William Edgar

ARTHUR WILLIAM EDGAR O'SHAUGHNESSY (1844–1881),
born in London, was educated privately and became
assistant in the natural history department of the British
Museum. In his *Epic of Women and other Poems*, 1870,
his great lyrical gift was shewn at its best.

Ode

WE are the music-makers,
    And we are the dreamers of dreams,
Wandering by lone sea-breakers,
    And sitting by desolate streams;—

[1] See Preface to this Anthology.

World-losers and world-forsakers,
  On whom the pale moon gleams:
Yet we are the movers and shakers
  Of the world for ever, it seems.

With wonderful deathless ditties
We build up the world's great cities,
  And out of a fabulous story
  We fashion an empire's glory:
One man with a dream, at pleasure,
  Shall go forth and conquer a crown;
And three with a new song's measure
  Can trample a kingdom down.

We, in the ages lying
  In the buried past of the earth,
Built Nineveh with our sighing,
  And Babel itself in our mirth;
And o'erthrew them with prophesying
  To the old of the new world's worth;
For each age is a dream that is dying,
  Or one that is coming to birth.

A breath of our inspiration
Is the life of each generation;
  A wondrous thing of our dreaming
  Unearthly, impossible seeming—
The soldier, the king, and the peasant
  Are working together in one,
Till our dream shall become their present,
  And their work in the world be done.

They had no vision amazing
Of the goodly house they are raising;
  They had no divine foreshowing
  Of the land to which they are going:
But on one man's soul it hath broken,
  A light that doth not depart;
And his look, or a word he hath spoken,
  Wrought flame in another man's heart.

And therefore to-day is thrilling
With a past day's late fulfilling;
　　And the multitudes are enlisted
　　In the faith that their fathers resisted,
And, scorning the dream of to-morrow,
　　Are bringing to pass, as they may,
In the world, for its joy or its sorrow,
　　The dream that was scorned yesterday.

But we, with our dreaming and singing,
　　Ceaseless and sorrowless we!
The glory about us clinging
　　Of the glorious future we see,
Our souls with high music ringing:
　　O men! it must ever be
That we dwell, in our dreaming and singing,
　　A little apart from ye.

For we are afar with the dawning
　　And the suns that are not yet high,
And out of the infinite morning
　　Intrepid you hear us cry—
How, spite of your human scorning,
　　Once more God's future draws nigh,
And already goes forth the warning
　　That ye of the past must die.

Great hail! we cry to the comers
　　From the dazzling unknown shore;
Bring us hither your sun and your summers,
　　And renew our world as of yore;
You shall teach us your song's new numbers,
　　And things that we dreamed not before:
Yea, in spite of a dreamer who slumbers,
　　And a singer who sings no more.

HOPKINS, Gerard Manley

GERARD MANLEY HOPKINS (1844–1889), born at Strat-
ford, Essex, was educated at Highgate School and Balliol
College, Oxford. He became a Jesuit in 1868, burning

what he had written. He published no verse; and to Robert Bridges we owe the collection *Poems of Gerard Manley Hopkins*, issued in 1918.

Pied Beauty

GLORY be to God for dappled things—
  For skies of couple-colour as a brinded cow;
    For rose-moles all in stipple upon trout that
      swim;
Fresh-firecoal chestnut-falls; finches' wings;
  Landscape plotted and pieced—fold, fallow and
    plóugh;
    And áll trádes, their gear and tackle and trim.

All things counter, original, spare, strange;
  Whatever is fickle, freckled (who knows how?)
    With swift, slow; sweet, sour; adazzle, dim;
He fathers-forth whose beauty is past change:
    Praise him.

LANG, Andrew

ANDREW LANG (1844–1912), born at Selkirk, educated at Selkirk Grammar School, the Edinburgh Academy, St Andrews University and Balliol College, Oxford, received a fellowship at Merton College, but resigned it to devote himself to journalism and literature. Greek scholar, student of history and of folklore, Lang was a most prolific prose writer and only secondarily a poet. But he will be remembered for one or two sonnets.

The Odyssey

As one that for a weary space has lain
  Lull'd by the song of Circe and her wine
  In gardens near the pale of Proserpine,
Where that Æaean isle forgets the main,
And only the low lutes of love complain,
  And only shadows of wan lovers pine;
  As such an one were glad to know the brine
Salt on his lips, and the large air again,—

So gladly, from the songs of modern speech
   Men turn, and see the stars, and feel the free
      Shrill wind beyond the close of heavy flowers;
    And, through the music of the languid hours,
They hear like ocean on the western beach
   The surge and thunder of the Odyssey.

BRIDGES, Robert Seymour

ROBERT SEYMOUR BRIDGES (O.M.) (1844–1930), born in
Thanet, was educated at Eton and Corpus Christi College,
Oxford. The study and practice of medicine filled the years
to 1882. Plays, critical essays on Milton and Keats and
poems appeared. In 1913 the Laureateship was conferred.
The Poetical Works of Robert Bridges was published in
1914. *The Spirit of Man* (an anthology of English and
French poetry and prose) was published during the War;
and more recent work, including *The Testament of Beauty*,
came from Bridges's pen. Few poets have shown so
much interest in prosody.

So sweet love seemed that April morn,
When first we kissed beside the thorn,
So strangely sweet, it was not strange
We thought that love could never change.

But I can tell—let truth be told—
That love will change in growing old;
Though day by day is nought to see,
So delicate his motions be.

And in the end 'twill come to pass
Quite to forget what once he was,
Nor even in fancy to recall
The pleasure that was all in all.

His little spring, that sweet we found,
So deep in summer floods is drowned,
I wonder, bathed in joy complete,
How love so young could be so sweet.

MEYNELL, Alice Christiana

ALICE CHRISTIANA MEYNELL (1847–1922), born in London, was educated by her father, T. J. Thompson. Much of her childhood was spent in Italy and she early became a convert to Roman Catholicism. In 1875, her first volume of poetry *Preludes*, which included *Renouncement*, appeared. Two years later she married Wilfrid Meynell. She wrote essays and journalistic articles. Francis Thompson was one of her many literary friends. Her complete *Poems* were published in 1923.

Renouncement

I MUST not think of thee; and, tired yet strong,
   I shun the thought that lurks in all delight—
     The thought of thee—and in the blue Heaven's
       height,
And in the sweetest passage of a song.

Oh, just beyond the fairest thoughts that throng
   This breast, the thought of thee waits, hidden yet
     bright;
     But it must never, never come in sight;
I must stop short of thee the whole day long.

But when sleep comes to close each difficult day,
   When night gives pause to the long watch I keep,
     And all my bonds I needs must loose apart,
Must doff my will as raiment laid away,—
   With the first dream that comes with the first sleep
     I run, I run, I am gathered to thy heart.

HENLEY, William Ernest

WILLIAM ERNEST HENLEY (1849–1903), born at Gloucester, was educated at the Crypt Grammar School there. Verse, written in an Edinburgh hospital, was sent to the *Cornhill*, whose editor, Leslie Stephen, accompanied by "R. L. S.," visited Henley. Henley became a journalist.

TO R. T. H. B.

OUT of the night that covers me,
   Black as the Pit from pole to pole,
I thank whatever gods may be
   For my unconquerable soul.

In the fell clutch of circumstance
    I have not winced nor cried aloud.
Under the bludgeonings of chance
    My head is bloody, but unbowed.

Beyond this place of wrath and tears
    Looms but the Horror of the shade,
And yet the menace of the years
    Finds, and shall find, me unafraid.

It matters not how strait the gate,
    How charged with punishments the scroll,
I am the master of my fate:
    I am the captain of my soul.

STEVENSON, Robert Louis

ROBERT LOUIS STEVENSON (1850–1894) was born in
Edinburgh. His education, at schools in Edinburgh and
at the University there, was irregular. Forced to give up
his father's profession of engineering, he studied law but
forsook it for literature. He travelled widely in quest of
health and met Henley, Leslie Stephen, Andrew Lang,
Edmund Gosse, George Meredith. *Treasure Island* made
him known to the general public in 1883. *A Child's
Garden of Verses* came out two years later. His reputation
was secured in 1886 by *The Strange Case of Dr Jekyll and
Mr Hyde* and *Kidnapped*. Another volume of poetry,
Underwoods, appeared. A yachting excursion in the
South Seas led to his settling in Samoa. There, in greatly
improved health, Stevenson wrote and worked among
the natives until his sudden death in 1894. The charm of
R. L. S. as a man has become legendary. Stevenson is
a prose stylist; his poetry is incidental, fresh and sincere.

> SING me a song of a lad that is gone,
>   Say, could that lad be I?
> Merry of soul he sailed on a day
>   Over the sea to Skye.
>
> Mull was astern, Rum on the port,
>   Eigg on the starboard bow;
> Glory of youth glowed in his soul:
>   Where is that glory now?

*　　　*　　　*

Give me again all that was there,
   Give me the sun that shone!
Give me the eyes, give me the soul,
   Give me the lad that's gone!

*   *   *

Billow and breeze, islands and seas,
   Mountains of rain and sun,
All that was good, all that was fair,
   All that was me is gone.

Requiem

UNDER the wide and starry sky,
Dig the grave and let me lie.
Glad did I live and gladly die
   And I laid me down with a will.

This be the verse you grave for me:
Here he lies where he longed to be,
Home is the sailor, home from sea,
   And the hunter home from the hill.

SHARP, William

WILLIAM SHARP (1856–1905), born at Paisley, was educated at Glasgow Academy and the University of Glasgow. Through Rossetti, he obtained a foothold in journalism. He wrote novels and verse in his own name. As "Fiona Macleod," he produced many Celtic stories, plays and poems, notably *The Immortal Hour*. "Fiona Macleod" became better known to the general public than did William Sharp. Though William Sharp's poem *Motherhood* needs the recension it never received, it is quite notable. William Sharp and "Fiona Macleod" appear to have nothing in common.

The Crescent Moon

As though the Power that made the nautilus
A living glory o'er seas perilous
Scathless to roam, had from the utmost deep
Called a vast flawless pearl from out its sleep
And carv'd it crescent-wise, exceeding fair,—
So seems the crescent moon that thro' the air

With motionless motion glides from out the west,
And sailing onward ever seems at rest.

WATSON, (Sir) William

WILLIAM WATSON—Knight—(1858–   ) was born at
Burley-in-Wharfedale and brought up in Liverpool.
The poem *Wordsworth's Grave*, 1890, secured the author
recognition. Other poems, from out of which *World-
Strangeness, Shelley's Centenary* and the *Father of the
Forest* are perhaps especially worth singling, reveal Sir
William as a poet practising a rare restraint and achieving
an all too uncommon grace of expression. He was
knighted in 1917 and receives a Civil List pension.

From *Wordsworth's Grave*

POET who sleepest by this wandering wave!
  When thou wast born, what birth-gift hadst thou
      then?
To thee what wealth was that the Immortals gave,
  The wealth thou gavest in thy turn to men?

Not Milton's keen, translunar music thine;
  Not Shakespeare's cloudless, boundless human
      view;
Not Shelley's flush of rose on peaks divine;
  Nor yet the wizard twilight Coleridge knew.

What hadst thou that could make so large amends
  For all thou hadst not and thy peers possessed,
Motion and fire, swift means to radiant ends?—
  Thou hadst, for weary feet, the gift of rest.

From Shelley's dazzling glow or thunderous haze,
  From Byron's tempest-anger, tempest-mirth,
Men turned to thee and found—not blast and blaze,
  Tumult of tottering heavens, but peace on earth.

Nor peace that grows by Lethe, scentless flower,
  There in white languors to decline and cease;
But peace whose names are also rapture, power,
  Clear sight, and love: for these are parts of peace.

World-Strangeness

STRANGE the world about me lies,
   Never yet familiar grown—
Still disturbs me with surprise,
   Haunts me like a face half known.

In this house with starry dome,
   Floored with gemlike plains and seas,
Shall I never feel at home,
   Never wholly be at ease?

On from room to room I stray,
   Yet my Host can ne'er espy,
And I know not to this day
   Whether guest or captive I.

So, betwixt the starry dome
   And the floor of plains and seas,
I have never felt at home,
   Never wholly been at ease.

The Inexorable Law

WE, too, shall pass; we, too, shall disappear,
Ev'n as the mighty nations that have waned
And perished. Not more surely are ordained
The crescence and the cadence of the year,
High-hearted June, October drooped and sere,
Than this gray consummation. We have reigned
Augustly; let our part be so sustained
That in far morns, whose voice we shall not hear,
It may be said: "This Mistress of the sword
And conquering prow, this Empire swol'n with
     spoils,
Yet served the Human Cause, yet strove for Man;
Hers was the purest greatness we record;
We whose ingathered sheaves her tilth foreran:
Whose Peace comes of her tempests, and her toils."

THOMPSON, Francis

FRANCIS THOMPSON (1859–1907), born at Preston, was educated at Ushaw College and at Owens College, Manchester, where he studied medicine but failed to pass his examinations. Reproached by his father for his inability to earn a living, he left home for London in 1885, suffered great privation and became, through neuralgia, an opium-taker. Given employment by a bootmaker, he wrote verse which he sent to Wilfrid Meynell. Meynell accepted it and, with his wife, befriended the poet. Thompson cured himself of opium-taking and regained some measure of health. 1893 saw his first volume, containing *The Hound of Heaven* which was widely praised. *Sister Songs*, dedicated to the Meynell children, came out, 1895, *New Poems*, 1897, the essay *Shelley* posthumously in 1908 in the *Dublin Review*. The poems *The Hound of Heaven*, *The Dead Cardinal*, and *O World Invisible*, are lofty achievements placing him in the van of English poets, quite overshadowing his minor Roman Catholic colleagues.

The Hound of Heaven

I FLED Him, down the nights and down the days;
I fled Him, down the arches of the years;
I fled Him, down the labyrinthine ways
Of my own mind; and in the mist of tears
I hid from Him, and under running laughter.
        Up vistaed hopes I sped;
        And shot, precipitated,
Adown Titanic glooms of chasmèd fears,
From those strong Feet that followed, followed
        after.
        But with unhurrying chase,
        And unperturbèd pace,
Deliberate speed, majestic instancy,
        They beat—and a Voice beat
        More instant than the Feet—
"All things betray thee, who betrayest Me."

I pleaded, outlaw-wise,
By many a hearted casement, curtained red,
    Trellised with intertwining charities;
(For, though I knew His love Who followèd,
        Yet was I sore adread
Lest, having Him, I must have naught beside).
But, if one little casement parted wide,
    The gust of His approach would clash it to.
    Fear wist not to evade, as Love wist to pursue.
Across the margent of the world I fled,
    And troubled the gold gateways of the stars,
    Smiting for shelter on their clangèd bars;
        Fretted to dulcet jars
And silvern chatter the pale ports o' the moon.
I said to Dawn: Be sudden—to Eve: Be soon;
    With thy young skiey blossoms heap me over
        From this tremendous Lover—
Float thy vague veil about me, lest He see!
    I tempted all His servitors, but to find
My own betrayal in their constancy,
In faith to Him their fickleness to me,
    Their traitorous trueness, and their loyal deceit.
To all swift things for swiftness did I sue;
    Clung to the whistling mane of every wind.
        But whether they swept, smoothly fleet,
    The long savannahs of the blue;
        Or whether, Thunder-driven,
    They clanged his chariot 'thwart a heaven
Plashy with flying lightnings round the spurn
        o' their feet:—
    Fear wist not to evade as Love wist to pursue.
        Still with unhurrying chase,
        And unperturbèd pace,
    Deliberate speed, majestic instancy,
        Came on the following Feet,
        And a Voice above their beat—
    "Naught shelters thee, who wilt not shelter
        Me."

I sought no more that after which I strayed
     In face of man or maid;
But still within the little children's eyes
     Seems something, something that replies,
They at least are for me, surely for me!
I turned me to them very wistfully;
But just as their young eyes grew sudden fair
     With dawning answers there,
Their angel plucked them from me by the hair.
"Come then, ye other children, Nature's—
        share
With me" (said I) "your delicate fellowship;
     Let me greet you lip to lip,
     Let me twine with you caresses,
        Wantoning
     With our Lady-Mother's vagrant tresses,
        Banqueting
     With her in her wind-walled palace
     Underneath her azured daïs,
     Quaffing, as your taintless way is,
        From a chalice
Lucent-weeping out of the dayspring."
        So it was done:
I in their delicate fellowship was one—
Drew the bolt of Nature's secrecies.
      I knew all the swift importings
      On the wilful face of skies;
      I knew how the clouds arise
      Spumèd of the wild sea-snortings;
        All that's born or dies
      Rose and drooped with; made them
        shapers
Of mine own moods, or wailful or divine;
      With them joyed and was bereaven.
      I was heavy with the even,
      When she lit her glimmering tapers
      Round the day's dead sanctities.
      I laughed in the morning's eyes.

I triumphed and I saddened with all weather,
         Heaven and I wept together,
And its sweet tears were salt with mortal mine;
Against the red throb of its sunset-heart
         I laid my own to beat,
         And share commingling heat;
But not by that, by that, was eased my human
         smart.
In vain my tears were wet on Heaven's grey cheek.
For ah! we know not what each other says,
         These things and I; in sound *I* speak—
Their sound is but their stir, they speak by silences.
Nature, poor stepdame, cannot slake my drouth;
         Let her, if she would owe me,
Drop yon blue bosom-veil of sky, and show me
         The breasts o' her tenderness:
Never did any milk of hers once bless
         My thirsting mouth.
         Nigh and nigh draws the chase,
         With unperturbèd pace,
     Deliberate speed, majestic instancy;
         And past those noisèd Feet
         A voice comes yet more fleet—
     "Lo! naught contents thee, who content'st
         not Me."

Naked I wait Thy love's uplifted stroke!
My harness piece by piece Thou hast hewn from
         me,
         And smitten me to my knee;
         I am defenceless utterly.
         I slept, methinks, and woke,
And, slowly gazing, find me stripped in sleep.
In the rash lustihead of my young powers,
         I shook the pillaring hours
And pulled my life upon me; grimed with smears,
I stand amid the dust o' the mounded years—
My mangled youth lies dead beneath the heap.

My days have crackled and gone up in smoke,
Have puffed and burst as sun-starts on a stream.
      Yea, faileth now even dream
The dreamer, and the lute the lutanist;
Even the linked fantasies, in whose blossomy twist
I swung the earth a trinket at my wrist,
Are yielding; cords of all too weak account
For earth with heavy griefs so overplussed.
      Ah! is Thy love indeed
A weed, albeit an amaranthine weed,
Suffering no flowers except its own to mount?
      Ah! must—
      Designer infinite!—
Ah! must Thou char the wood ere Thou canst limn
      with it?
My freshness spent its wavering shower i' the dust;
And now my heart is as a broken fount,
Wherein tear-drippings stagnate, spilt down ever
      From the dank thoughts that shiver
Upon the sighful branches of my mind.
      Such is; what is to be?
The pulp so bitter, how shall taste the rind?
I dimly guess what Time in mists confounds;
Yet ever and anon a trumpet sounds
From the hid battlements of Eternity;
Those shaken mists a space unsettle, then
Round the half-glimpsèd turrets slowly wash again.
      But not ere him who summoneth
      I first have seen, enwound
With glooming robes purpureal, cypress-crowned;
His name I know, and what his trumpet saith.
Whether man's heart or life it be which yields
      Thee harvest, must Thy harvest fields
      Be dunged with rotten death?

      Now of that long pursuit
      Comes on at hand the bruit;
That Voice is round me like a bursting sea:

"And is thy earth so marred,
    Shattered in shard on shard?
Lo, all things fly thee, for thou fliest Me!
  Strange, piteous, futile thing!
Wherefore should any set thee love apart?
Seeing none but I makes much of naught" (He said),
"And human love needs human meriting:
    How hast thou merited—
Of all man's clotted clay the dingiest clot?
    Alack, thou knowest not
How little worthy of any love thou art!
Whom wilt thou find to love ignoble thee,
    Save Me, save only Me?
All which I took from thee I did but take,
    Not for thy harms,
But just that thou might'st seek it in My arms.
    All which thy child's mistake
Fancies as lost, I have stored for thee at home:
  Rise, clasp My hand, and come!"

    Halts by me that footfall:
    Is my gloom, after all,
Shade of His hand, outstretched caressingly?
  "Ah, fondest, blindest, weakest,
  I am He Whom thou seekest!
Thou dravest love from thee, who dravest Me."

The Kingdom of God

"In no strange land"

O WORLD invisible, we view thee,
O world intangible, we touch thee,
O world unknowable, we know thee,
Inapprehensible, we clutch thee!

Does the fish soar to find the ocean,
The eagle plunge to find the air—
That we ask of the stars in motion
If they have rumour of thee there?

Not where the wheeling systems darken,
And our benumbed conceiving soars!—
The drift of pinions, would we hearken,
Beats at our own clay-shuttered doors.

The angels keep their ancient places;—
Turn but a stone, and start a wing!
'Tis ye, 'tis your estrangèd faces,
That miss the many-splendoured thing.

But (when so sad thou canst not sadder)
Cry;—and upon thy so sore loss
Shall shine the traffic of Jacob's ladder
Pitched betwixt Heaven and Charing Cross.

Yea, in the night, my Soul, my daughter,
Cry,—clinging Heaven by the hems;
And lo, Christ walking on the water
Not of Genesareth, but Thames!

HOUSMAN, Alfred Edward

ALFRED EDWARD HOUSMAN (1859–   ) was educated
at Bromsgrove School and St John's College, Oxford.
He has had a distinguished career as classical scholar
and professor at London and Cambridge. A volume of
lyrics *A Shropshire Lad* came out in 1896. *Last Poems*,
1922, appealed to a wide public. They have a classical
perfection of style and simplicity of theme.

Epitaph on an Army of Mercenaries

THESE, in the day when heaven was falling,
　　The hour when earth's foundations fled,
Followed their mercenary calling
　　And took their wages and are dead.

Their shoulders held the sky suspended;
　　They stood, and earth's foundations stay;
What God abandoned, these defended,
　　And saved the sum of things for pay.

SEAMAN, (Sir) Owen

OWEN SEAMAN—Knight—(1861–   ) was born in London. He was educated at Shrewsbury and Clare College, Cambridge. After teaching at Rossall, he became Professor of Literature at the College of Science, Newcastle. His connection with *Punch* began in 1894. Twelve years later he became editor, and in 1914 he was knighted. His clever verse is an almost weekly delight.

To William Shakspeare

[For the occasion of the Historic Costume
Ball given in his honour.]

SWIFT falls to some the meed of high renown;
  At eve their fame is *nil*; they've not begun it;
Next morning they're the talk of half the Town—
  A column in *The Daily* —— has done it;
But, ere the country came to understand
  That *your* performance furnished ample reason
    For pomps of so superb a brand,
    It took them just three centuries and
      A Coronation Season.

But now the Smart Contingent "takes you up";
  For you, the very last of London's crazes,
Society consents to dance and sup—
  The noblest monument it ever raises;
Not theirs to question—that were too abstruse—
  Whether your actual merit more or less is,
    But, like a charity, your use
    Is to afford a fit excuse
      For wearing fancy dresses.

Thus in their dinner-parties forth they go,
  Plumed and brocaded, wigged and precious-
        stony—
Rosalind, *Portia*, *Puck* and *Prospero*,
  Strikingly reproducing your *personæ*;

123

All times and scenes—from *Hamlet's* Elsinore
　　To *Juliet's* "fair Verona" (quattro-cento),
　　　　Making for you, from out their store
　　　　Of rather vague historic lore,
　　　　　　A truly *chic* memento.

Master, if such affairs intrigue your ghost
　　Moving at large among the world's immortals,
You'll guess what motive bids this gallant host
　　Swarm to the masquerade through ALBERT'S
　　　　　　portals.
Is it your show or theirs? Of such a doubt
　　Your human wit will make a healthy clearance;
　　　　You'll judge that all who join the rout
　　　　Are solely exercised about
　　　　　　Their personal appearance.

And yet—God speed them at their "SHAKSPEARE
　　　　Ball",
　　Treading (on others' toes) the daedal dances,
Though some have never read your plays at all,
　　And some imagine you are BACON (FRANCIS);
They serve an end; their ticket-money buys
　　Solid material for the shrine we owe you;
　　　　Some day a temple's walls may rise
　　　　Where, even under English skies,
　　　　　　People may get to know you.

NEWBOLT, (Sir) Henry John

HENRY JOHN NEWBOLT—Knight—(1862–　　), born at
Bilston, Staffordshire, was educated at Clifton College and
Corpus Christi College, Oxford. He practised as a barrister
for twelve years. His ballads, *Admirals All*, made his
reputation. Other volumes of verse followed, notably
Drake's Drum and Other Sea Songs (1914). In 1915, the
author was knighted. He completed (Sir) Julian Corbett's
editorship of the official Admiralty *History of the Great
War*. His verse is stirring and patriotic.

Drake's Drum

DRAKE he's in his hammock an' a thousand mile
    away,
  (Capten, art tha sleepin' there below?),
Slung atween the round shot in Nombre Dios Bay,
  An' dreamin' arl the time o' Plymouth Hoe.
Yarnder lumes the Island, yarnder lie the ships,
  Wi' sailor lads a-dancin' heel-an'-toe,
An' the shore-lights flashin', an' the night-tide
    dashin',
  He sees et arl so plainly as he saw et long ago.

Drake he was a Devon man, an' rüled the Devon
    seas,
  (Capten, art tha sleepin' there below?),
Rovin' tho' his death fell, he went wi' heart at
    ease,
  An' dreamin' arl the time o' Plymouth Hoe.
"Take my drum to England, hang et by the shore,
  Strike et when your powder's runnin' low;
If the Dons sight Devon, I'll quit the port
    o' Heaven,
  An' drum them up the Channel as we drummed
    them long ago."

Drake he's in his hammock till the great Armadas
    come,
  (Capten, art tha sleepin' there below?),
Slung atween the round shot, listenin' for the drum,
  An' dreamin' arl the time o' Plymouth Hoe.
Call him on the deep sea, call him up the Sound,
  Call him when ye sail to meet the foe;
Where the old trade's plyin' an' the old flag flyin'
  They shall find him ware an' wakin', as they
    found him long ago!

The Fighting Téméraire

It was eight bells ringing,
  For the morning watch was done,
And the gunner's lads were singing
  As they polished every gun.
It was eight bells ringing,
And the gunner's lads were singing,
For the ship she rode a-swinging
  As they polished every gun.

  Oh! to see the linstock lighting,
    Téméraire! Téméraire!
  Oh! to hear the round shot biting,
    Téméraire! Téméraire!
  Oh! to see the linstock lighting,
  And to hear the round shot biting,
  For we're all in love with fighting
    On the Fighting Téméraire.

It was noontide ringing,
  And the battle just begun,
When the ship her way was winging
  As they loaded every gun.
It was noontide ringing,
When the ship her way was winging,
And the gunner's lads were singing
  As they loaded every gun.

  There'll be many grim and gory,
    Téméraire! Téméraire!
  There'll be few to tell the story,
    Téméraire! Téméraire!
  There'll be many grim and gory,
  There'll be few to tell the story,
  But we'll all be one in glory
    With the Fighting Téméraire.

There's a far bell ringing
  At the setting of the sun,
And a phantom voice is singing
  Of the great days done.
There's a far bell ringing,
And a phantom voice is singing
Of renown for ever clinging
  To the great days done.

Now the sunset breezes shiver,
  Téméraire! Téméraire!
And she's fading down the river,
  Téméraire! Téméraire!
Now the sunset breezes shiver,
And she's fading down the river,
But in England's song for ever
  She's the Fighting Téméraire.

JACOB, Violet

Violet Jacob (1863–   ) was born near Montrose and educated privately. She has published novels and collections of verse.

Tam i' the Kirk

O Jean, my Jean, when the bell ca's the congregation
  Owre valley an' hill wi' the ding frae its iron mou',
When a' body's thochts is set on his ain salvation,
  Mine's set on you.

There's a reid rose lies on the Buik o' the Word 'afore ye
  That was growin' braw on its bush at the keek o' day,
But the lad that pu'd yon flower i' the mornin's glory,
  He canna pray.

He canna pray; but there's nane i' the Kirk will
heed him
Whaur he sits sae still his lane at the side of the
wa',
For nane but the reid rose kens what my lassie
gie'd him,
It an' us twa!

He canna sing for the sang that his ain he'rt raises,
He canna see for the mist that's afore his een,
And a voice drouns the hale o' the psalms an' the
paraphrases,
Cryin' "Jean, Jean, Jean!"

KIPLING, Rudyard

RUDYARD KIPLING (1865–   ) was born at Bombay and
educated at the United Services College, Westward Ho,
North Devon. He took up journalistic work in India,
travelled the world. A long list of publications, prose and
verse, stands to his credit. *Barrack Room Ballads*,
Stalky & Co., *Kim*, *The Five Nations*, *Puck of Pook's
Hill* and *Fringes of the Fleet* are among the best known of
his works. The volume *Inclusive Verse* yields the readiest
approach to his poetry. The Nobel prize has been accorded the author. His style is unique and arresting.

The Land

FRIENDLY BROOK

WHEN Julius Fabricius, Sub-Prefect of the Weald,
In the days of Diocletian owned our Lower River-
field,
He called to him Hobdenius—a Briton of the Clay,
Saying: "What about that River-piece for layin' in
to hay?"

And the aged Hobden answered: "I remember as
a lad
"My father told your father that she wanted dreenin'
bad.

"An' the more that you neeglect her the less you'll
    get her clean.
"Hev it jest *as* you've a mind to, but, if I was you,
    I'd dreen."

So they drained it long and crossways in the lavish
    Roman style.
Still we find among the river-drift their flakes of
    ancient tile,
And in drouthy middle August, when the bones of
    meadows show,
We can trace the lines they followed sixteen hun-
    dred years ago.

Then Julius Fabricius died as even Prefects do,
And after certain centuries Imperial Rome died
    too.
Then did robbers enter Britain from across the
    Northern main
And our Lower River-field was won by Ogier the
    Dane.

Well could Ogier work his war-boat—well could
    Ogier wield his brand—
Much he knew of foaming waters—not so much of
    farming land.
So he called to him a Hobden of the old unaltered
    blood,
Saying: "What about that River-piece; she doesn't
    look no good?"

And that aged Hobden answered: "'Tain't for *me*
    to interfere,
"But I've known that bit o' meadow now for five
    and fifty year.
"Hev it *jest* as you've a mind to, but I've proved it
    time on time,
"If you want to change her nature you have *got* to
    give her lime!"

Ogier sent his wains to Lewes, twenty hours'
    solemn walk,
And drew back great abundance of the cool, grey,
    healing chalk.
And old Hobden spread it broadcast, never heeding
    what was in't.—
Which is why in cleaning ditches, now and then we
    find a flint.

Ogier died. His sons grew English—Anglo-Saxon
    was their name—
Till out of blossomed Normandy another pirate
    came;
For Duke William conquered England and divided
    with his men,
And our Lower River-field he gave to William of
    Warenne.

But the Brook (you know her habit) rose one rainy
    autumn night
And tore down sodden flitches of the bank to left
    and right.
So, said William to his Bailiff as they rode their
    dripping rounds:
"Hob, what about that River-bit—the Brook's got
    up no bounds?"

And that aged Hobden answered: "'Tain't my
    business to advise,
"But ye might ha' known 'twould happen from the
    way the valley lies.
"When ye can't hold back the water you must try
    and save the sile,
"Hev it jest as you've a *mind* to, but, if I was you,
    I'd spile!"

They spiled along the water-course with trunks of
    willow-trees,
And planks of elms behind 'em and immortal oaken
    knees.

And when the spates of Autumn whirl the gravel-
beds away
You can see their faithful fragments iron-hard in
iron clay.

*   *   *   *

Georgii Quinti Anno Sexto, I, who own the River-
field,
Am fortified with title-deeds, attested, signed and
sealed,
Guaranteeing me, my assigns, my executors and
heirs
All sorts of powers and profits which—are neither
mine nor theirs.

I have rights of chase and warren, as my dignity
requires.
I can fish—but Hobden tickles. I can shoot—but
Hobden wires.
I repair, but he reopens, certain gaps which, men
allege,
Have been used by every Hobden since a Hobden
swapped a hedge.

Shall I dog his morning progress o'er the track-
betraying dew?
Demand the dinner-basket into which my pheasant
flew?
Confiscate his evening faggot under which the
conies ran,
And summons him to judgment? I would sooner
summons Pan.

His dead are in the churchyard—thirty generations
laid.
Their names were old in history when Domesday
Book was made;
And the passion and the piety and prowess of his line
Have seeded, rooted, fruited in some land the Law
calls mine.

Not for any beast that burrows, not for any bird
    that flies,
Would I lose his large sound counsel, miss his keen
    amending eyes.
He is bailiff, woodman, wheelwright, field-sur-
    veyor, engineer,
And if flagrantly a poacher—'tain't for me to
    interfere.

"Hob, what about that River-bit?" I turn to him
    again,
With Fabricius and Ogier and William of Warenne.
"Hev it jest as you've a mind to, *but*"—and here he
    takes command.
For whoever pays the taxes old Mus' Hobden owns
    the land.

Mine Sweepers

DAWN off the Foreland—the young flood making
    Jumbled and short and steep—
Black in the hollows and bright where it's breaking—
    Awkward water to sweep.
    "Mines reported in the fairway,
    "Warn all traffic and detain.
"'Sent up *Unity, Claribel, Assyrian, Stormcock*, and
    Golden Gain."

Noon off the Foreland—the first ebb making
    Lumpy and strong in the bight.
Boom after boom, and the golf-hut shaking
    And the jackdaws wild with fright!
    "Mines located in the fairway,
    "Boats now working up the chain.
"Sweepers—*Unity, Claribel, Assyrian, Stormcock*,
    and *Golden Gain*."

Dusk off the Foreland—the last light going
  And the traffic crowding through,
And five damned trawlers with their syreens blowing
  Heading the whole review!
  "Sweep completed in the fairway.
  "No more mines remain.
"'Sent back *Unity, Claribel, Assyrian, Stormcock,*
  and *Golden Gain.*"

YEATS, William Butler

WILLIAM BUTLER YEATS (1865–), born at Sandymount,
near Dublin, was educated at the Godolphin School,
Hammersmith, and Erasmus Smith School, Dublin. He
studied art but turned to literature. He began to establish
a reputation with the publication of the poetic drama *The
Countess Cathleen*, 1892. Two years later, the similar
drama *The Land of Heart's Desire* appeared. Considerable
later work has been added; and, to the annoyance of some
critics, the author is constantly revising. Mr Yeats was
associated with Lady Gregory in the foundation of the
Abbey Theatre, Dublin. It is a happy fortune that Mr
Yeats has written in the English tongue. He is leader of
Irish letters and has received the Nobel prize.

The Lake Isle of Innisfree

I WILL arise and go now, and go to Innisfree,
And a small cabin build there, of clay and wattles
    made:
Nine bean rows will I have there, a hive for the
    honey-bee,
  And live alone in the bee-loud glade.

And I shall have some peace there, for peace comes
    dropping slow,
Dropping from the veils of the morning to where
    the cricket sings;
There midnight's all a glimmer, and noon a purple
    glow,
  And evening full of the linnet's wings.

I will arise and go now, for always night and day
I hear lake water lapping with low sounds by the
    shore;
While I stand on the roadway, or on the pavements
    gray,
  I hear it in the deep heart's core.

DOWSON, Ernest

ERNEST DOWSON (1867–1900), born at Lee, Kent, was
educated chiefly out of England and at Queen's College,
Oxford. He left without taking a degree. Drink ruined
his life; he died in poverty. Dowson's lyrical gift was
real; but he had little to say.

Vitae summa brevis spem nos vetat incohare longam

THEY are not long, the weeping and the laughter,
  Love and desire and hate;
I think they have no portion in us after
  We pass the gate.

They are not long, the days of wine and roses:
  Out of a misty dream
Our path emerges for a while, then closes
  Within a dream.

GALSWORTHY, John

JOHN GALSWORTHY (O.M.) (1867–   ) was born on
Kingston Hill, Surrey, and educated at Harrow and New
College, Oxford. Though called to the Bar he turned to
literature. *The Man of Property*, the first novel of the now
famous "Forsyte Saga," appeared in 1906. In 1906 also
the drama *The Silver Box* was published. A series of
plays including *Strife*, *Justice*, *The Skin Game* and
Loyalties attest the author's greatness in writing for the
stage. He rightly enjoys a wide popularity here and
abroad—not least in Germany.

Unknown

You who had worked in perfect ways
To turn the wheel of nights and days,
Who coaxed to life each running rill
And froze the snow-crown on the hill,
The cold, the starry flocks who drove,
And made the circling seasons move;
How came your jesting purpose when
You fashioned monkeys into men?

You who invented peacock's dress—
You, Lord of cruel happiness!—
Who improvised all flight and song
And loved and killed the whole day long,
And filled with colour to the brim
The cup of your completed whim!
What set you frolicking when we
Were given power to feel and see?

Why not have kept the stellar plan
Quite soulless and absolved from man?
What heavy need to make this thing—
A monkey with an angel's wing;
A murderous poor saint, who reaps
His fields of death, and, seeing—weeps?
No! If the saffron day could sigh
And sway *unconscious*—Why am I?

*　　*　　*　　*

Unknown! You slept one afternoon
And dreamed, and turned, and woke too soon!
The sorrel glowed, and the bees hummed,
And Mother Nature's fingers strummed,
And flock of dandelion was blown,
And the yew-trees cast their shadows down.
Such beauty seemed to you forlorn—
And lo!—this playboy, Man, was born!

PHILLIPS, Stephen

STEPHEN PHILLIPS (1864–1915) was born at Summertown, near Oxford, and educated in Stratford-on-Avon, at King's School, Peterborough, and at Oundle School. He joined the theatrical company of his cousin (Sir) Frank Benson. *Poems*, 1898, including *Christ in Hades* and *Marpessa*, established his reputation as a narrative writer. With the production by (Sir) H. Beerbohm Tree of *Herod*, 1900, and of *Paolo and Francesca*, 1902, by (Sir) George Alexander, Phillips leapt to fame. Sir Owen Seaman's opinion of *Paolo and Francesca* "something without parallel in our age" was shared by such critics as W. L. Courtney and William Archer. The drama *Ulysses* and other work followed. Wealth slipped through Phillips' hands. Phillips is a Marlowe touched by the introspection of a later century.

From *Paolo and Francesca*

Part of ACT I

Enter LUCREZIA. *She touches* GIOVANNI *on the arm.*

Luc.   Pardon me—you sit alone.
While there is time, I have stolen in on you
To speak my dearest wishes for this marriage,
And in a manner, too, old friend, farewell.
   Gio. Farewell?
   Luc.   And in a manner 'tis farewell.
   Gio. This marriage is political.
   Luc.   No more?
   Gio. And yet since I have seen Francesca, I
Have fallen into a trance. It seems, indeed,
That I am bringing into this dark air
A pureness that shall purge these ancient halls.
   Luc. Watch, then, this pureness: fend it fearfully.
   Gio. I took her dreaming from her convent trees.
   Luc. And for that reason tremble at her more
Old friend, remember that we two are passed
Into the grey of life: but O, beware
This child scarce yet awake upon the world
Dread her first ecstasy, if one should come
That should appear to her half-opened eyes

Wonderful as a prince from fairyland
Or venturing through forests toward her face—
No—do not stride about the room—your limp
Is evident the more—come, sit by me
As you were wont to sit. Youth goes toward youth.
  Gio. What peril can be here? In Rimini?
  Luc. I have but said and say, "Youth goes toward
      youth,"
And she shall never prize, as I do still,
Your savage courage and deliberate force,
Even your mounded back and sullen gait.
  Gio. Lucrezia! this is that old bitterness.
  Luc. Bitterness—am I bitter? Strange, O strange!
How else? My husband dead and childless left,
My thwarted woman-thoughts have inward turned,
And that vain milk like acid in me eats.
Have I not in my thought trained little feet
To venture, and taught little lips to move
Until they shaped the wonder of a word?
I am long practised. O those children, mine!
Mine, doubly mine: and yet I cannot touch them,
I cannot see them, hear them—Does great God
Expect I shall clasp air and kiss the wind
For ever? And the budding cometh on,
The burgeoning, the cruel flowering:
At night the quickening splash of rain, at dawn
That muffled call of babes how like to birds;
And I amid these sights and sounds must starve—
I, with so much to give, perish of thrift!
Omitted by His casual dew!
  Gio.   Well, well,
You are spared much: children can wring the heart.
  Luc. Spared! to be spared what I was born to have!
I am a woman, and this very flesh
Demands its natural pangs, its rightful throes,
And I implore with vehemence these pains.
I know that children wound us, and surprise
Even to utter death, till we at last

Turn from a face to flowers: but this my heart
Was ready for these pangs, and had foreseen.
O! but I grudge the mother her last look
Upon the coffined form—that pang is rich—
Envy the shivering cry when gravel falls.
And all these maiméd wants and thwarted thoughts,
Eternal yearning, answered by the wind,
Have dried in me belief and love and fear.
I am become a danger and a menace,
A wandering fire, a disappointed force,
A peril—do you hear, Giovanni?—O!
It is such souls as mine that go to swell
The childless cavern cry of the barren sea,
Or make that human ending to night-wind.
Why have I bared myself to you?—I know not,
Unless, indeed, this marriage—yes, this marriage—
Near now, is't not?—So near made me cry out.
Ah! she will bring a sound of pattering feet!
But now this message—and those papers. I
Must haste to see the banquet-table spread—
Your bride is yet so young.   [*Exit Lucrezia*
  Gio. [*reads*]   "Antonio
And Conti urge it is impolitic
To lay another load"—Youth goes toward youth!—
"On murmuring Pesaro"—in Rimini!—
"Foresee revolt." Here in the house all's safe.

Part of ACT IV

[FRANCESCA *alone*.] *Enter* PAOLO

  Pao. I am by music led into this room,
And beckoned sweetly: all the breezes die
Round me, and in immortal ecstasy
Toward thee I move: now am I free and gay—
Light as a dancer when the strings begin.
  Franc. What glow is on thy face, what sudden light?
  Pao. It seems that I am proof against all perils.
  Franc. And yet I fear to see thy air so glad.

138

Pao. To-night all points of swords to me are dull.
Franc. And still I dread the bravery of your words.
Kiss me, and leave me, Paolo, to-night.
Pao. What do you fear?
Franc.   One watches quietly.
Pao. Who?
Franc.   I know not: perhaps the quiet face
Of God: the eternal Listener is near.
  Pao. I'll struggle now no more. Have I not
        fought
Against thee as a foe most terrible?
Parried the nimble thrust and thought of thee,
And from thy mortal sweetness fled away,
Yet evermore returned? Now all the bonds
Which held me I cast off—honour, esteem,
All ties, all friendships, peace, and life itself.
You only in this universe I want.
  Franc. You fill me with a glorious rashness. What!
Shall we two, then, take up our fate and smile?
  Pao. Remember how when first we met we stood
Stung with immortal recollections.
O face immured beside a fairy sea,
That leaned down at dead midnight to be kissed!
O beauty folded up in forests old!
Thou wast the lovely quest of Arthur's knights—
  Franc. Thy armour glimmered in a gloom of green.
  Pao. Did I not sing to thee in Babylon?
  Franc. Or did we set a sail in Carthage bay?
  Pao. Were thine eyes strange?
  Franc.   Did I not know thy voice?
All ghostly grew the sun, unreal the air
Then when we kissed.
  Pao.   And in that kiss our souls
Together flashed, and now they are one flame,
Which nothing can put out, nothing divide.
  Franc. Kiss me again! I smile at what may chance.
  Pao. Again, and yet again! and here and here.
Let me with kisses burn this body away,
That our two souls may dart together free.

I fret at intervention of the flesh,
And I would clasp you—you that but inhabit
This lovely house.

   Franc.   Break open then the door,
And let my spirit out. Paolo, kill me!
Then kill thyself: to vengeance leave these weeds,
And let our souls together soar away.

   Pao. [*recoiling*]. You are too beautiful for human
        blow!   [*Francesca starts*
Why did you shiver and turn sudden cold?

   Franc. [*slowly*]. I felt a wind pass over me.

   Pao.   I too:
Colder than any summer night could give.

   Franc. A solitary wind: and it hath passed.

   Pao. [*Embracing her*]. Do you still fear?

   Franc.   Ah, Paolo! if we
Should die to-night, then whither would our souls
Repair? There is a region which priests tell of
Where such as we are punished without end.

   Pao. Were we together, what can punish us?

   Franc. Nothing! Ah! think not I can love you less—
Only I fear.

   Pao.   What can we fear, we two?
O God, Thou seest us Thy creatures bound
Together by that law which holds the stars
In palpitating cosmic passion bright;
By which the very sun enthrals the earth,
And all the waves of the world faint to the moon.
Even by such attraction we two rush
Together through the everlasting years.
Us, then, whose only pain can be to part,
How wilt Thou punish? For what ecstasy
Together to be blown about the globe!
What rapture in perpetual fire to burn
Together!—where we are is endless fire.
There centuries shall in a moment pass,
And all the cycles in one hour elapse!
Still, still together, even when faints Thy sun,

And past our souls Thy stars like ashes fall,
How wilt Thou punish us who cannot part?
   Franc. I lie out on your arm and say your name—
"Paolo!" "Paolo!"
   Pao.   "Francesca!"

Shakespeare

I

OTHERS have pictured thee as mild and bland,
And of a cloudless boundless human view;
Of calm regard and of composure grand,
To whom was nothing strange, and nothing new.
Not thus do I conceive thee; but as one
That bitterly exclaimed on human doom,
And as a spirit sad beneath the sun,
And dreading a worse thing beyond the tomb.
Man but "an angry ape" appeared; who fed
With torment laughter of the gods on high;
Lear on the heath, Othello by the bed
Awakened but the mockery of the sky.
And ah! in this dark welter of the soul
No guide art thou and urgest to no goal.

II

O true that thou couldst warble pastoral bliss,
Of forest and green field and fairy land,
Since to thy boundless reach nought came amiss,
Thou to the nearest task didst set thy hand.
And yet thy deepest hour was vast despair,
And the true mood of thee was dark and fell;
Then heaven with human lightning didst thou bare,
Thy thunder echoed in the pools of hell.
A sunny smiler all with God at rest,
This would they have thee for thy lighter strain.
To me a rebel dost thou stand confest,
With mighty mutiny of heart and brain;
And in no vale of Arden thy renown,
But accusation of the heavens thy crown.

BINYON, Laurence

LAURENCE BINYON (1869–   ) was born at Lancaster and educated at St Paul's School and Trinity College, Oxford. He is Deputy Keeper in charge of Oriental prints and drawings at the British Museum; and, apart from producing valuable catalogues and criticism, has written many plays and poems. *The Four Years* contains War poems. In editing *The Golden Treasury of Modern Lyrics* the poet has placed all lovers of poetry under obligation.

For the Fallen

WITH proud thanksgiving, a mother for her children,
England mourns for her dead across the sea.
Flesh of her flesh they were, spirit of her spirit,
Fallen in the cause of the free.

Solemn the drums thrill: Death august and royal
Sings sorrow up into immortal spheres.
There is music in the midst of desolation
And a glory that shines upon our tears.

They went with songs to the battle, they were young,
Straight of limb, true of eye, steady and aglow.
They were staunch to the end against odds uncounted,
They fell with their faces to the foe.

They shall grow not old, as we that are left grow old:
Age shall not weary them, nor the years condemn.
At the going down of the sun and in the morning
We will remember them.

They mingle not with their laughing comrades again;
They sit no more at familiar tables at home;
They have no lot in our labour of the day-time;
They sleep beyond England's foam.

But where our desires are and our hopes profound,
Felt as a well-spring that is hidden from sight,
To the innermost heart of their own land they are
    known
As the stars are known to the Night;

As the stars that shall be bright when we are dust,
Moving in marches upon the heavenly plain,
As the stars that are starry in the time of our dark-
    ness,
To the end, to the end, they remain.

HODGSON, Ralph

RALPH HODGSON (1872–   ) was born in Yorkshire,
lived in America, became a journalist in London and
afterwards lecturer in poetry at the Tohoku University,
Sendai, Japan. Mr Hodgson's published verse reveals a
great love of animals.

The Bells of Heaven

'TWOULD ring the bells of Heaven
The wildest peal for years,
If Parson lost his senses
And people came to theirs,
And he and they together
Knelt down with angry prayers
For tamed and shabby tigers
And dancing dogs and bears,
And wretched, blind pit ponies,
And little hunted hares.

DE LA MARE, Walter

WALTER DE LA MARE (1873–   ) was born of Huguenot
ancestry at Charlton, Kent, and educated at St Paul's
Cathedral Choir School. For a while he engaged in
business. *Henry Brocken*, a novel, appeared in 1904. A
Privy Purse grant enabled the author to develop literary
work. *The Listeners and other Poems*, 1912, and *Peacock
Pie*, 1913, are widely known. In 1920 *Collected Poems*,

1901–1918, appeared. The writing of Mr de la Mare is of new and strange quality, by the phantasy of which the reader is gladly held captive. He is the rarest dreamer of our age.

Nod

SOFTLY along the road of evening,
    In a twilight dim with rose,
Wrinkled with age, and drenched with dew,
    Old Nod, the shepherd, goes.

His drowsy flock streams on before him,
    Their fleeces charged with gold,
To where the sun's last beam leans low
    On Nod the shepherd's fold.

The hedge is quick and green with briar,
    From their sand the conies creep;
And all the birds that fly in heaven
    Flock singing home to sleep.

His lambs outnumber a noon's roses,
    Yet, when night's shadows fall,
His blind old sheep-dog, Slumber-soon,
    Misses not one of all.

His are the quiet steeps of dreamland,
    The waters of no-more-pain,
His ram's bell rings 'neath an arch of stars,
    "Rest, rest, and rest again."

Off the Ground

THREE jolly Farmers
    Once bet a pound
Each dance the others would
    Off the ground.
Out of their coats
    They slipped right soon,
And neat and nicesome
    Put each his shoon.

One—Two—Three!—
   And away they go,
Not too fast,
   And not too slow;
Out from the elm-tree's
   Noonday shadow,
Into the sun
   And across the meadow.
Past the schoolroom,
   With knees well bent
Fingers a-flicking,
   They dancing went.
Up sides and over,
   And round and round,
They crossed click-clacking
   The Parish bound,
By Tupman's meadow
   They did their mile,
Tee-to-tum
   On a three-barred stile.
Then straight through Whipham,
   Downhill to Week,
Footing it lightsome,
   But not too quick,
Up fields to Watchet
   And on through Wye,
Till seven fine churches
   They'd seen skip by—
Seven fine churches,
   And five old mills,
Farms in the valley,
   And sheep on the hills;
Old Man's Acre
   And Dead Man's Pool
All left behind,
   As they danced through Wool.
And Wool gone by,
   Like tops that seem

To spin in sleep
  They danced in dream:
Withy—Wellover—
  Wassop—Wo—
Like an old clock
  Their heels did go.
A league and a league
  And a league they went,
And not one weary,
  And not one spent.
And lo, and behold!
  Past Willow-cum-Leigh
Stretched with its waters
  The great green sea.
Says Farmer Bates,
  "I puffs and I blows,
What's under the water,
  Why, no man knows!"
Says Farmer Giles,
  "My wind comes weak,
And a good man drownded
  Is far to seek."
But Farmer Turvey,
  On twirling toes
Up's with his gaiters,
  And in he goes:
Down where the mermaids
  Pluck and play
On their twangling harps
  In a sea-green day;
Down where the mermaids,
  Finned and fair,
Sleek with their combs
  Their yellow hair. . . .
Bates and Giles
  On the shingle sat,
Gazing at Turvey's
  Floating hat.

But never a ripple
  Nor bubble told
Where he was supping
  Off plates of gold.
Never an echo
  Rilled through the sea
Of the feasting and dancing
  And minstrelsy.
They called—called—called:
  Came no reply:
Nought but the ripples'
  Sandy sigh.
Then glum and silent
  They sat instead,
Vacantly brooding
  On home and bed,
Till both together
  Stood up and said:—
"Us knows not, dreams not,
  Where you be,
Turvey, unless
  In the deep blue sea;
But axcusing silver—
  And it comes most willing—
Here's us two paying
  Our forty shilling;
For it's sartin sure, Turvey,
  Safe and sound,
You danced us square, Turvey,
  Off the ground!"

Silver

SLOWLY, silently, now the moon
Walks the night in her silver shoon;
This way, and that, she peers, and sees
Silver fruit upon silver trees;
One by one the casements catch
Her beams beneath the silvery thatch;

Couched in his kennel, like a log,
With paws of silver sleeps the dog;
From their shadowy cote the white breasts peep
Of doves in a silver-feathered sleep;
A harvest mouse goes scampering by,
With silver claws, and silver eye;
And moveless fish in the waters gleam,
By silver reeds in a silver stream.

BOTTOMLEY, Gordon

GORDON BOTTOMLEY (1874–   ) was born at Keighley
and educated at Keighley Grammar School. He is the
author of much verse and strong and original drama.
King Lear's Wife and *Gruach* are, probably, his finest
plays. His *Poems of Thirty Years* appeared in 1925.

Calvary-Talk

THREE black crosses against the sky;
A sun like a bubble of blood;
A cawing rook with lifted wings
Poised on the middle rood.

A moaning corpse on either hand,
A silent Corpse between
Sagging with sharp protruding knees
And chin on bosom lean.

The rabble had gone. The Westered sun
Dropped like a dead man's head,
Who raising himself for a last look
Slips back upon the bed.

Three men sat there, and as they talked
By a watch-fire newly lit
Their monstrous shadows flung on the beam
Hid the limp Corpse on it.

(They crouched and crept, they reeled and leapt,
Then sank in a smoky flare
That lit the shapeless hanging mouth
And lank dark-dripping hair.)

One was the man who stretched the limbs
With the clutch of a long-dreamed sin,
One was the man who held the nails
While the third man knocked them in.

"At noon we tossed for the Preacher's shirt
Sodden with blood and sweat:
I sold the sorry rag to a woman
Whose face was drawn and wet.

"Now some men thieve and some men stab
And know what the end will be,
So whether they sing or twist or curse
Upon the sapless tree
As the big nails crush the little bones
Does not matter to me.

"They lie and cheat, they take their chance,
They know the loser pays;
So whether they die with prayers and sobs
Or the brag of the brazen face,
I glory in God as the points go through,
A minister of grace.

"But to nail a rough-tongued prophet up,
A harmless drone and clean—
You might have wiped the shame from my face
As I drove the cold nails in;
'Twas only work for priests or their wives,
For men too spiteful and mean."

The hammer-man spat; the nail-man donned
His share of Jesus' clothing;
The limb-man cried, "'Twas the surgeons' hate,—
He healed their sick, and for nothing."

Up the hill and over the hill
With cloths on a bier spread,
The pitiful mourners came again
Who thought their God was dead.

From *King Lear's Wife*

[Goneril to Hygd—her mother]

GONERIL. Then I shall lull you, as you once lulled me.
    [*Seating herself on the bed, she sings*
    The owlets in roof holes
    Can sing for themselves;
    The smallest brown squirrel
    Both scampers and delves;
    But a baby does nothing—
    She never knows how—
    She must hark to her mother
    Who sings to her now.
    Sleep then, ladykin, peeping so;
    Hide your handies and ley lei lo.
    [*She bends over* HYGD *and kisses her;*
    they laugh softly together
LEAR *parts the curtains of the door at the back, stands*
 there a moment, then goes away noiselessly.
    The lish baby otter
    Is sleeky and streaming,
    With catching bright fishes,
    Ere babies learn dreaming;
    But no wet little otter
    Is ever so warm
    As the fleecy-wrapt baby
    'Twixt me and my arm.
    Sleep big mousie...
HYGD, *suddenly irritable.* Be quiet...I cannot bear
it.
    [*She turns her head away from*
    GONERIL *and closes her eyes*

CHESTERTON, Gilbert Keith

GILBERT KEITH CHESTERTON (1874–   ), born in London, was educated at St Paul's School. Entering journalism he won a reputation as a brilliant political propagandist, defending and abandoning Liberalism and Socialism in turn. He has written much literary criticism, much fiction—his "Father Brown" series of detective stories is noted—two plays—one of which is *Magic*—and verse. Since 1922 he has professed Roman Catholicism and, with the weapon of paradox, continues to wage an amusing warfare.

The Donkey

WHEN fishes flew and forests walked
    And figs grew upon thorn,
Some moment when the moon was blood
    Then surely I was born.

With monstrous head and sickening cry
    And ears like errant wings,
The devil's walking parody
    On all four-footed things.

The tattered outlaw of the earth,
    Of ancient crooked will;
Starve, scourge, deride me: I am dumb,
    I keep my secret still.

Fools! For I also had my hour;
    One far fierce hour and sweet;
There was a shout about my ears,
    And palms before my feet.

TAYLOR, Rachel Annand

RACHEL ANNAND TAYLOR (1876–   ) was born in
Aberdeen, attended schools and studied at the University
there. She has published poems and criticism; but is,
perhaps, most widely known as a reviewer of novels in
The Spectator.

The Quietist

I DREAMED as dream the seraphim
   Where God's white roses grew.
Then, lest I caitiff were to Him,
   I ran to draw and hew
With them that labour. So my guilt
   Seemed over; but askew
I clove the wood, and ever spilt
   The water that I drew.
   And bitter was my rue.

Then came the Master of Delight
   And softly called for me:
"Be still, be still, mine acolyte!
   My dreams are laid on thee.
It is enough, it is enough
   To hearken and to see
The secret sweetest things of Love,
   And waft felicity,—
   Yea! like a white rose-tree."

MASEFIELD, John

JOHN MASEFIELD (1878–   ) was born at Ledbury,
Herefordshire, and trained for the sea on the *Conway*
in the Mersey. He served before the mast. The play *The
Tragedy of Nan* and the fine narrative poems *The Everlasting Mercy*, *The Widow in the Bye Street*, *Dauber*, a
tale of the seas, *The Daffodil Fields* established a reputation
which later work, including novels, has enhanced. It is
safe to predict that Mr Masefield will go down to posterity
as a master of English realism. On the death of Bridges
in 1930 the Laureateship was conferred on Mr Masefield.

Cargoes

QUINQUIREME of Nineveh from distant Ophir
Rowing home to haven in sunny Palestine,
With a cargo of ivory,
And apes and peacocks,
Sandalwood, cedarwood, and sweet white wine.

Stately Spanish galleon coming from the Isthmus,
Dipping through the Tropics by the palm-green
    shores,
With a cargo of diamonds,
Emeralds, amethysts,
Topazes, and cinnamon, and gold moidores.

Dirty British coaster with a salt-caked smoke stack
Butting through the Channel in the mad March
    days,
With a cargo of Tyne coal,
Road-rail, pig-lead,
Firewood, iron-ware, and cheap tin trays.

Beauty

I HAVE seen dawn and sunset on moors and windy
    hills
Coming in solemn beauty like slow old tunes of
    Spain:
I have seen the lady April bringing the daffodils,
Bringing the springing grass and the soft warm
    April rain.

I have heard the song of the blossoms and the old
    chant of the sea,
And seen strange lands from under the arched
    white sails of ships;
But the loveliest things of beauty God ever has
    showed to me,
Are her voice, and her hair, and eyes, and the dear
    red curve of her lips.

From *Fragments*

Troy Town is covered up with weeds,
  The rabbits and the pismires brood
On broken gold, and shards, and beads
  Where Priam's ancient palace stood.

The floors of many a gallant house
  Are matted with the roots of grass;
The glow-worm and the nimble mouse
  Among her ruins flit and pass.

And there, in orts of blackened bone,
  The widowed Trojan beauties lie,
And Simois babbles over stone
  And waps and gurgles to the sky.

Once there were merry days in Troy,
  Her chimneys smoked with cooking meals,
The passing chariots did annoy
  The sunning housewives at their wheels.

And many a lovely Trojan maid
  Set Trojan lads to lovely things;
The game of life was nobly played,
  They played the game like Queens and Kings.

So that, when Troy had greatly passed
  In one red roaring fiery coal,
The courts the Grecians overcast
  Became a city in the soul.

From *The Widow in the Bye Street*

They walked to town, Jim on the blacksmith's arm.
Jimmy was crying like a child, and saying,
"I never meant to do him any harm."
His teeth went clack, like bones at murmurs
    playing,
And then he trembled hard and broke out praying,

"God help my poor old mother. If he's dead,
I've brought her my last wages home," he said.

He trod his last free journey down the street;
Treading the middle road, and seeing both sides,
The school, the inns, the butchers selling meat,
The busy market where the town divides.
Then past the tanpits full of stinking hides,
And up the lane to death, as weak as pith.
"By God, I hate this, Jimmy," said the smith.

     *   *   *   *

Anna in black, the judge in scarlet robes,
A fuss of lawyers' people coming, going,
The windows shut, the gas alight in globes,
Evening outside, and pleasant weather blowing.
"They'll hang him?" "I suppose so; there's no
         knowing."
"A pretty piece, the woman, ain't she, John?
He killed the fellow just for carrying on."

"She give her piece to counsel pretty clear."
"Ah, that she did, and when she stop she smiled."
"She's had a-many men, that pretty dear;
She's drove a-many pretty fellows wild."
"More silly idiots they to be beguiled."
"Well, I don't know." "Well, I do. See her eyes?
Mystery, eh? A woman's mystery's lies."

     *   *   *   *

Guilty. Thumbs down. No hope. The judge passed
         sentence;
"A frantic passionate youth, unfit for life,
A fitting time afforded for repentance,
Then certain justice with a pitiless knife.
For her his wretched victim's widowed wife,
Pity. For her who bore him, pity. (Cheers.)
The jury were exempt for seven years."

All bowed; the Judge passed to the robing room,
Dismissed his clerks, disrobed, and knelt and prayed
As was his custom after passing doom,
Doom upon life, upon the thing not made.
"O God, who made us out of dust, and laid
Thee in us bright, to lead us to the truth,
O God, have pity upon this poor youth.

"Show him Thy grace, O God, before he die;
Shine in his heart; have mercy upon me,
Who deal the laws men make to travel by
Under the sun upon the path to Thee;
O God, Thou knowest I'm as blind as he,
As blind, as frantic, not so single, worse,
Only Thy pity spared me from the curse."

*   *   *   *

Jimmy was taken down into a cell,
He did not need a hand, he made no fuss.
The men were kind "for what the kid done...well
The same might come to any one of us."
They brought him bits of cake at tea time: thus
The love that fashioned all in human ken,
Works in the marvellous hearts of simple men.

*   *   *   *

There was a group outside the prison gate,
Waiting to hear them ring the passing bell,
Waiting as empty people always wait
For the strong toxic of another's hell.
And mother stood there, too, not seeing well,
Praying through tears to let His will be done,
And not to hide His mercy from her son.

Talk in the little group was passing quick.
"It 's nothing now to what it was, to watch."
"Poor wretched kid, I bet he 's feeling sick."
"Eh? What d'you say, chaps? Someone got a
    match?"
"They draw a bolt and drop you down a hatch

And break your neck, whereas they used to strangle
In olden times, when you could see them dangle."

Some one said "Off hats" when the bell began.
Mother was whimpering now upon her knees.
A broken ringing like a beaten pan
It sent the sparrows wavering to the trees.
The wall-top grasses whickered in the breeze,
The broken ringing clanged, clattered and clanged
As though men's bees were swarming, not men
      hanged.

Now certain Justice with the pitiless knife.
The white sick chaplain snuffling at the nose,
"I am the resurrection and the life."
The bell still clangs, the small procession goes,
The prison warders ready ranged in rows.
"Now, Gurney, come, my dear; it's time," they
      said.
And ninety seconds later he was dead.

          *   *   *   *

She tottered home, back to the little room,
It was all over for her, but for life;
She drew the blinds, and trembled in the gloom;
"I sat here thus when I was wedded wife;
Sorrow sometimes, and joy; but always strife,
Struggle to live except just at the last.
O God, I thank Thee for the mercies past.

"Harry, my man, when we were courting; eh...
The April morning up the Cony-gree.
How grand he looked upon our wedding day.
'I wish we'd had the bells,' he said to me;
And we'd the moon that evening, I and he,
And dew come wet, oh, I remember how,
And we come home to where I'm sitting now.

"And he lay dead here, and his son was born here;
He never saw his son, his little Jim.
And now I'm all alone here, left to mourn here,
And there are all his clothes, but never him.
He's down under the prison in the dim,
With quicklime working on him to the bone,
The flesh I made with many and many a groan.

"Oh, how his little face come, with bright hair,
Dear little face. We made this room so snug;
He sit beside me in his little chair,
I give him real tea sometimes in his mug.
He liked the velvet in the patchwork rug.
He used to stroke it, did my pretty son,
He called it Bunny, little Jimmie done.

"And then he ran so, he was strong at running,
Always a strong one, like his dad at that.
In summertimes I done my sewing sunning,
And he'd be sprawling, playing with the cat.
And neighbours brought their knitting out to chat
Till five o'clock; he had his tea at five;
How sweet life was when Jimmy was alive!"

THOMAS, Philip Edward

PHILIP EDWARD THOMAS (1878–1917), born in Lambeth,
of Welsh and Spanish descent, was educated at St Paul's
School and Lincoln College, Oxford. He became a
journalist—an excellent writer of nature studies. Six
months before the war, Thomas began to write poetry.
In 1915, he enlisted and two years later was killed at
Arras. The *Collected Poems of Edward Thomas* appeared
in 1920; in a foreword Mr de la Mare spoke of the
poet's "impassioned, almost trance-like delight in things
natural."

Adlestrop

YES. I remember Adlestrop—
The name, because one afternoon
Of heat the express-train drew up there
Unwontedly. It was late June.

The steam hissed. Some one cleared his throat.
No one left and no one came
On the bare platform. What I saw
Was Adlestrop—only the name

And willows, willow-herb, and grass,
And meadowsweet, and haycocks dry,
No whit less still and lonely fair
Than the high cloudlets in the sky.

And for that minute a blackbird sang
Close by, and round him, mistier,
Farther and farther, all the birds
Of Oxfordshire and Gloucestershire.

WEBB, Mary

MARY WEBB (1881–1927), born at Leighton, Shropshire,
of Welsh and Scotch ancestry, was educated at home and
at Southport. She took to novel writing. Though the
quality of her work had for years been recognised by
such writers as Mr de la Mare, it needed the praise
of a Prime Minister, Mr Stanley Baldwin, to commend
her novels to the general public. Probably, *Precious Bane*
is the most popular. Her verse, posthumously published,
is still too little known. It consists of lyrics often exquisite in style, which shew an extraordinary observation
of the countryside. Mary Webb, however, was no mere
descriptive writer but a true nature mystic.

Farewell to Beauty

"Their being is to be perceived"—BERKELEY

LET fall your golden showers, laburnum tree!
Break the grey casket of your buds for me—
Soon I shall go where never gold is seen,
And who will be with you as I have been?

Quick with your silver notes, O silver bird!
Wistful, I listen for the song I heard
Many a day, but soon shall hear no more,
For summoning winds are out along the shore.

All things so early fade—swiftly pass over,
As autumn bees desert the withering clover.
Now, with the bee, I sing immortal June;
How soon both song and bee are gone—how soon!

Who'll watch the clover secretly unclose?
Finger the sycamore buds, afire with rose?
Trace the mauve veins of the anemone?
Know the peculiar scent of every tree?

Maybe the solemn hill, the enchanted plain
Will be but arable and wild again,
Losing the purple bloom they wore for me—
The dreaming god I could so clearly see.

DRINKWATER, John

JOHN DRINKWATER (1882–   ) was born at Leytonstone,
Essex, and educated at Oxford High School. He turned
from insurance business to theatrical production and
management, inaugurating the Birmingham Repertory
Theatre. He became famous in England and America
through the authorship of the fine play *Abraham Lincoln*.
Further plays—including *Mary Stuart*—poems—*Collected Poems*, 1923—and criticisms of Byron and C. J. Fox,
have appeared.

Birthright

LORD Rameses of Egypt sighed
    Because a summer evening passed;
And little Ariadne cried
    That summer fancy fell at last
To dust; and young Verona died
    When beauty's hour was overcast.

Theirs was the bitterness we know
    Because the clouds of hawthorn keep
So short a state, and kisses go
    To tombs unfathomably deep,
While Rameses and Romeo
    And little Ariadne sleep.

FLECKER, Herman (James) Elroy

JAMES ELROY FLECKER (1884–1915), born in Lewisham, was educated at Dean Close School, Cheltenham, Uppingham and Trinity College, Oxford. In 1907, he went to London. After teaching for a short while, he entered Caius College, Cambridge, studying Oriental languages for the Consular service. Flecker was sent to Constantinople, but he was forced by ill-health to return to England. Seemingly recovered, he went back to his post, and was transferred to Beirut, where he spent two years before being compelled by consumption to remove to Switzerland. In 1913, *The Golden Journey to Samarkand* appeared. Flecker died at Davos in 1915. *The Old Ships* came out, posthumously, in 1915. Mr Squire issued Flecker's *Collected Poems* a year later. *Hassan*, published in 1922, was unforgettably staged by Mr Basil Dean at His Majesty's, 1923. If Flecker's early death cut short a career of great promise, it is certain that, in the haunting music of the *Golden Journey to Samarkand* and the Oriental splendour of *Hassan*, Flecker, poet and dramatist, makes a unique and undeniable claim to fame.

To a Poet a Thousand Years Hence

I WHO am dead a thousand years,
    And wrote this sweet archaic song,
Send you my words for messengers
    The way I shall not pass along.

I care not if you bridge the seas,
    Or ride secure the cruel sky,
Or build consummate palaces
    Of metal or of masonry.

But have you wine and music still,
    And statues and a bright-eyed love,
And foolish thoughts of good and ill,
    And prayers to them who sit above?

How shall we conquer? Like a wind
    That falls at eve our fancies blow,
And old Mæonides the blind
    Said it three thousand years ago.

O friend unseen, unborn, unknown,
  Student of our sweet English tongue,
Read out my words at night, alone:
  I was a poet, I was young.

Since I can never see your face,
  And never shake you by the hand,
I send my soul through time and space
  To greet you. You will understand.

From *Hassan*

ACT V, SC. II

*At the Gate of the Moon, Bagdad. Blazing moon-
light.* MERCHANTS, CAMEL-DRIVERS *and their beasts,*
PILGRIMS, JEWS, WOMEN, *all manner of people. By
the barred gate stands the* WATCHMAN *with a great
key. Among the pilgrims* HASSAN *and* ISHAK *in the
robes of pilgrims.*

THE MERCHANTS

(*Together*)
Away, for we are ready to a man!
  Our camels sniff the evening and are glad.
Lead on, O Master of the Caravan,
  Lead on the Merchant-Princes of Bagdad.

THE CHIEF DRAPER

Have we not Indian carpets dark as wine,
  Turbans and sashes, gowns and bows and veils,
And broideries of intricate design,
  And printed hangings in enormous bales?

THE CHIEF GROCER

We have rose-candy, we have spikenard,
  Mastic and terebinth and oil and spice,
And such sweet jams meticulously jarred
  As God's Own Prophet eats in Paradise.

THE PRINCIPAL JEWS

And we have manuscripts in peacock styles
  By Ali of Damascus: we have swords
Engraved with storks and apes and crocodiles,
  And heavy beaten necklaces for lords.

THE MASTER OF THE CARAVAN

But you are nothing but a lot of Jews.

PRINCIPAL JEW

Sir, even dogs have daylight, and we pay.

MASTER OF THE CARAVAN

But who are ye in rags and rotten shoes,
  You dirty-bearded, blocking up the way?

ISHAK

We are the Pilgrims, master; we shall go
  Always a little further: it may be
Beyond that last blue mountain barred with snow
  Across that angry or that glimmering sea,

White on a throne or guarded in a cave
  There lives a prophet who can understand
Why men were born: but surely we are brave,
  Who take the Golden Road to Samarkand.

THE CHIEF MERCHANT

We gnaw the nail of hurry. Master, away!

ONE OF THE WOMEN

O turn your eyes to where your children stand.
Is not Bagdad the beautiful? O, stay!

MERCHANTS

(*In chorus*)
  We take the Golden Road to Samarkand.

AN OLD MAN

Have you not girls and garlands in your homes,
  Eunuchs and Syrian boys at your command?
Seek not excess: God hateth him who roams!

MERCHANTS

(*In chorus*)
  We take the Golden Road to Samarkand.

HASSAN

Sweet to ride forth at evening from the wells,
  When shadows pass gigantic on the sand,
And softly through the silence beat the bells
  Along the Golden Road to Samarkand.

ISHAK

We travel not for trafficking alone;
  By hotter winds our fiery hearts are fanned:
For lust of knowing what should not be known,
  We take the Golden Road to Samarkand.

THE MASTER OF THE CARAVAN
Open the gate, O watchman of the night!

THE WATCHMAN

  Ho, travellers, I open. For what land
Leave you the dim-moon city of delight?

MERCHANTS

(*With a shout*)
  We take the Golden Road to Samarkand!
            (*The Caravan passes through the gate.*)

WATCHMAN

(*Consoling the women*)
What would ye, ladies? It was ever thus.
  Men are unwise and curiously planned.

A WOMAN

They have their dreams, and do not think of us.
            (*The* WATCHMAN *closes the gate.*)

VOICES OF THE CARAVAN

In the distance singing)
  We take the Golden Road to Samarkand.

CURTAIN

The Old Ships

I HAVE seen old ships sail like swans asleep
Beyond the village which men still call Tyre,
With leaden age o'ercargoed, dipping deep
For Famagusta and the hidden sun
That rings black Cyprus with a lake of fire;
And all those ships were certainly so old
Who knows how oft with squat and noisy gun,
Questing brown slaves or Syrian oranges,
The pirate Genoese
Hell-raked them till they rolled
Blood, water, fruit and corpses up the hold.
But now through friendly seas they softly run,
Painted the mid-sea blue or shore-sea green,
Still patterned with the vine and grapes in gold.

But I have seen,
Pointing her shapely shadows from the dawn
And image tumbled on a rose-swept bay,
A drowsy ship of some yet older day;
And, wonder's breath indrawn,
Thought I—who knows—who knows—but in that
      same
(Fished up beyond Æҽa, patched up new
—Stern painted brighter blue—)
That talkative, bald-headed seaman came
(Twelve patient comrades sweating at the oar)
From Troy's doom-crimson shore,
And with great lies about his wooden horse
Set the crew laughing, and forgot his course.

It was so old a ship—who knows, who knows?
—And yet so beautiful, I watched in vain
To see the mast burst open with a rose,
And the whole deck put on its leaves again.

SASSOON, Siegfried Loraine

SIEGFRIED LORAINE SASSOON (1886–   ), born at Mat-
field, Kent, was educated at Marlborough and Clare
College, Cambridge. In *Memoirs of an Infantry Officer*,
1930, he tells, under a thin disguise, his experiences on
the Western Front. *Selected Poems*, 1925, provides the
readiest approach to his verse.

"*They*"

THE Bishop tells us: "When the boys come back
They will not be the same; for they'll have fought
In a just cause: they lead the last attack
On Anti-Christ; their comrades' blood has bought
New right to breed an honourable race.
They have challenged Death and dared him face to
    face."

"We're none of us the same!" the boys reply.
"For George lost both his legs: and Bill's stone
    blind;
Poor Jim's shot through the lungs and like to die:
And Bert's gone syphilitic: you'll not find
A chap who's served that hasn't found *some*
    change."
And the Bishop said: "The ways of God are
    strange!"

Memorial Tablet (*Great War*)

SQUIRE nagged and bullied till I went to fight
(Under Lord Derby's scheme). I died in hell—
(They called it Passchendaele); my wound was
    slight,
And I was hobbling back, and then a shell
Burst slick upon the duck-boards; so I fell
Into the bottomless mud, and lost the light.

In sermon time, while Squire is in his pew,
He gives my gilded name a thoughtful stare;
For though low down upon the list, I'm there:
"In proud and glorious memory"—that's my due.

Two bleeding years I fought in France for Squire;
I suffered anguish that he's never guessed:
Once I came home on leave; and then went west.
What greater glory could a man desire?

BROOKE, Rupert

RUPERT BROOKE (1887–1915) was born at Rugby and educated at Rugby School and King's College, Cambridge, of which college he became a fellow. He served in the R.N.V.R. during the War, dying of blood-poisoning at Scyros. A volume of his poems was published in 1911, another after his death. His was the true promise of poesy.

The Hill

BREATHLESS, we flung us on the windy hill,
    Laughed in the sun, and kissed the lovely grass.
    You said, "Through glory and ecstasy we pass;
Wind, sun, and earth remain, the birds sing still,
When we are old, are old...". "And when we die
    All's over that is ours; and life burns on
Through other lovers, other lips," said I,
    "Heart of my heart, our heaven is now, is won!"

"We are Earth's best, that learnt her lesson here.
    Life is our cry. We have kept the faith!" we said;
    "We shall go down with unreluctant tread
Rose-crowned into the darkness!..." Proud we
        were,
And laughed, that had such brave true things to say.
—And then you suddenly cried, and turned away.

The Soldier

IF I should die, think only this of me:
    That there's some corner of a foreign field
That is for ever England. There shall be
    In that rich earth a richer dust concealed;
A dust whom England bore, shaped, made aware,
    Gave, once, her flowers to love, her ways to roam,
A body of England's, breathing English air,
    Washed by the rivers, blest by suns of home.

And think, this heart, all evil shed away,
  A pulse in the eternal mind, no less
      Gives somewhere back the thoughts by
          England given;
Her sights and sounds; dreams happy as her day;
  And laughter, learnt of friends; and gentleness,
      In hearts at peace, under an English heaven.

TURNER, Walter James Redfern

WALTER JAMES REDFERN TURNER (1889–   ), born in
China, was educated in Melbourne, Munich and Vienna.
His fantastic tragi-comedy *The Man who ate the Popo-
mack* came out in 1922.

Romance

WHEN I was but thirteen or so,
  I went into a golden land,
Chimborazo, Cotopaxi
  Took me by the hand.

My father died, my brother too,
  They passed like fleeting dreams,
I stood where Popocatapetl
  In the sunlight gleams.

I dimly heard the master's voice
  And boys far off at play,
Chimborazo, Cotopaxi
  Had stolen me away.

I walked in a great golden dream
  To and fro from school—
Shining Popocatapetl
  The dusty streets did rule.

I walked home with a gold dark boy
  And never a word I'd say,
Chimborazo, Cotopaxi
  Had taken my speech away.

I gazed entranced upon his face
   Fairer than any flower—
O shining Popocatapetl,
   It was thy magic hour.

The houses, people, traffic seemed
   Thin fading dreams by day,
Chimborazo, Cotopaxi,
   They had stolen my soul away!

POMEROY, Florence Mary

FLORENCE MARY POMEROY (1892–   ) was born of
Devonshire parentage in Hull. She was educated at the
Girls' High School there and in Orleans and graduated
at the University of London. Her published work is
journalistic.

Ad Naturam

Lines written upon reading *The Universe Around Us* by
Sir James Jeans

THOU hast no part in our brief hopes and fears,
No sympathy, as poets feign, with man!
Beyond the hollow tumult of our years
Thou art impersonal, mechanic plan,
Flame and the dark.... "In thee we live...." and
      die!
We are as foam scarce-moving waters throw
To the last daylight of an ocean sky,
Motes i' the sunbeam; as the waning bow
Arching dim hills! ...And this insentient tale
—Dawn, eve, returning dawn, bud, bursting bloom,
High profligate summer's perfumed ending day,
Now at the starlit hour, this nightingale?
I take thy gift, live, love, accept my doom
—One with the circling planets which decay!

SORLEY, Charles Hamilton

CHARLES HAMILTON SORLEY (1895–1915) was born in
Aberdeen and educated at King's College Choir School
and Marlborough. In December 1913 he gained a
scholarship to University College, Oxford. He visited
Germany, returning immediately before the outbreak of
the Great War. He received an infantry commission and
fell at Halluch. *Marlborough and other Poems* was
published in 1916.

The Song of the Ungirt Runners

WE swing ungirded hips,
And lightened are our eyes,
The rain is on our lips,
We do not run for prize.
We know not whom we trust
Nor whitherward we fare,
But we run because we must
    Through the great wide air.

The waters of the seas
Are troubled as by storm.
The tempest strips the trees
And does not leave them warm.
Does the tearing tempest pause?
Do the tree-tops ask it why?
So we run without a cause
    'Neath the big bare sky.

The rain is on our lips,
We do not run for prize.
But the storm the water whips
And the wave howls to the skies.
The winds arise and strike it
And scatter it like sand,
And we run because we like it
    Through the broad bright land.

BLUNDEN, Edmund Charles

EDMUND CHARLES BLUNDEN (1896–   ), born in London, was educated at Christ's Hospital and Queen's College, Oxford. He soldiered in the Great War. From 1924 to 1927, he was Professor of English Literature, Tokio University. Since 1916 he has published much verse and prose.

Almswomen

At Quincey's moat the squandering village ends,
And there in the almshouse dwell the dearest friends
Of all the village, two old dames that cling
As close as any trueloves in the spring.
Long, long ago they passed threescore-and-ten,
And in this doll's house lived together then;
All things they have in common, being so poor,
And their one fear, Death's shadow at the door.
Each sundown makes them mournful, each sunrise
Brings back the brightness in their failing eyes.

How happy go the rich fair-weather days
When on the roadside folk stare in amaze
At such a honeycomb of fruit and flowers
As mellows round their threshold; what long hours
They gloat upon their steepling hollyhocks,
Bee's balsams, feathery southernwood, and stocks,
Fiery dragon's-mouths, great mallow leaves
For salves, and lemon-plants in bushy sheaves,
Shagged Esau's-hands with five green finger-tips.
Such old sweet names are ever on their lips.
As pleased as little children where these grow
In cobbled pattens and worn gowns they go,
Proud of their wisdom when on gooseberry shoots
They stuck eggshells to fright from coming fruits
The brisk-billed rascals; pausing still to see
Their neighbour owls saunter from tree to tree,
Or in the hushing half-light mouse the lane
Long-winged and lordly.

But when these hours wane
Indoors they ponder, scared by the harsh storm
Whose pelting saracens on the window swarm,
And listen for the mail to clatter past
And church clock's deep bay withering on the blast;
They feed the fire that flings a freakish light
On pictured kings and queens grotesquely bright,
Platters and pitchers, faded calendars
And graceful hour-glass trim with lavenders.

Many a time they kiss and cry, and pray
That both be summoned in the selfsame day,
And wiseman linnet tinkling in his cage
End too with them the friendship of old age,
And all together leave their treasured room
Some bell-like evening when the may's in bloom.

INDEX OF FIRST LINES

A good sword and a trusty hand! . . *page* 8
A spirit seems to pass 102
A thousand summers ere the time of Christ . 47
Airly Beacon, Airly Beacon 63
As one that for a weary space has lain . . 109
As though the Power that made the nautilus . 113
At Quincey's moat the squandering village ends . 171
Awake! for Morning in the Bowl of Night . . 19
Away, for we are ready to a man! . . . 162

Break, break, break 44
Breathless, we flung us on the windy hill . . 167

Dawn off the Foreland—the young flood making 132
Does the road wind up-hill all the way? . . 86
Drake he's in his hammock an' a thousand mile
    away 125

Fear death?—to feel the fog in my throat . . 60
Flower o' the rose 55

Glory be to God for dappled things . . . 109
Go, for they call you, shepherd, from the hill . 76

Had she come all the way for this . . . 89
Helen, thy beauty is to me 18
Here, in this little Bay 83
Here, where the world is quiet . . . 96
How do I love thee? Let me count the ways . 10

I am by music led into this room . . . 138
I dreamed as dream the seraphim . . . 152
I fled Him, down the nights and down the days . 116
I have seen dawn and sunset on moors and windy
    hills 153

I have seen old ships sail like swans asleep . *page* 165
I must not think of thee; and, tired yet strong . 111
I who am dead a thousand years . . 161
I will arise and go now, and go to Innisfree . 133
If I should die, think only this of me . . . 167
If the red slayer think he slays . . . 9
In the heroic days when Ferdinand . . . 12
It little profits that an idle king . . . 42
It was eight bells ringing 126

Jenny kissed me when we met 1
Just for a handful of silver he left us . . 53

King Philip had vaunted his claims . . . 99

Let fall your golden showers, laburnum tree! . 159
Lord Rameses of Egypt sighed 160

My heart is like a singing bird 85

No coward soul is mine 61
Now sleeps the crimson petal, now the white . 45

O Jean, my Jean, when the bell ca's the congrega-
    tion 127
O world invisible, we view thee 121
Oh, to be in England 54
Oh! wherefore come ye forth, in triumph from the
    North 4
On either side the water lie . . . 32
Only a man harrowing clods 103
Others have pictured thee as mild and bland . 141
Out of the night that covers me . . . 111

Pardon me—you sit alone 136
Poet who sleepest by this wandering wave! . 114

Quinquireme of Nineveh from distant Ophir . 153

Say not, the struggle nought availeth . . 62
Sing me a song of a lad that is gone . . . 112
Slowly, silently, now the moon . . . 147

So here hath been dawning . . . *page* 3
So, on the bloody sand, Sohrab lay dead . . 75
So sweet love seemed that April morn . . 110
Softly along the road of evening . . . 144
Squire nagged and bullied till I went to fight . 166
Strange the world about me lies . . . 115
Strew on her roses, roses 74
Sunset and evening star 49
Swift falls to some the meed of high renown . 123

Tears, idle tears, I know not what they mean . 44
The Bishop tells us: "When the boys come back 166
The feathers of the willow 87
The out-spread world to span . . . 71
The mountain sheep are sweeter . . . 2
The old mayor climbed the belfry tower . . 65
The wish, that of the living whole . . . 46
The world rolls round for ever like a mill . . 88
The year's at the spring 53
Then I shall lull you, as you once lulled me . 150
There is sweet music here that softer falls . . 37
There's heaven above, and night by night . 51
These, in the day when heaven was falling . 122
They are not long, the weeping and the laughter 134
They walked to town, Jim on the blacksmith's arm 154
Think thou and act; tomorrow thou shalt die . 84
This is the ship of pearl, which, poets feign . 49
This is the weather the cuckoo likes . . . 104
Thou hast no part in our brief hopes and fears . 169
Three black crosses against the sky . . . 148
Three jolly Farmers 144
To Thee whose eye all Nature owns . . . 105
Troy Town is covered up with weeds . . 154
'Twould ring the bells of Heaven . . . 143

Under the wide and starry sky 113

We are the music-makers 106
We swing ungirded hips 170
We, too, shall pass; we, too, shall disappear . 115
Welcome, wild North-easter! 63
What was he doing, the great god Pan . . 10

175

When fishes flew and forests walked . . *page* 151
When I am dead, my dearest 85
When I was but thirteen or so 168
When Julius Fabricius, Sub-Prefect of the Weald 128
When the hounds of spring are on winter's traces 94
When the Present has latched its postern behind
    my tremulous stay 103
William Dewy, Tranter Reuben, Farmer Ledlow
    late at plough 100
With proud thanksgiving, a mother for her
    children 142

Yes. I remember Adlestrop 158
You promise heavens free from strife . . 82
You who had worked in perfect ways . . 135

9 781107 494428